KURSK DOWN! is the first complete story of the disaster and includes an inside-Russia look at the political calamity that ensued.

KURSK DOWN! provides information from translated official Russian Navy reports on the accident, then shows how details in this material have been altered to put the best face on actions taken by naval leaders.

KURSK DOWN! features exclusive interviews with rescuers.

KURSK DOWN! reveals the real reason behind the loss of this great vessel and her brave crew.

KURSK DOWN! conclusively proves what the Russian Navy was so loath to publicly admit—that an enormous explosion on board the *Kursk* sealed her fate.

THE FIRST BOOK
ON THE MARITIME DISASTER OF
THE DECADE.
AND THE ONLY BOOK
THAT GIVES YOU THE *REAL* STORY.

KURSK DOWN!

The Shocking True Story of the Sinking of a Russian Nuclear Submarine

CLYDE BURLESON

WARNER BOOKS

An AOL Time Warner Company

WARNER BOOKS EDITION

Copyright © 2002 by Clyde Burleson

Cover design by Diane Luger
Cover photography by Tony Greco

Warner Books, Inc.
1271 Avenue of the Americas
New York, NY 10020

Visit our Web site at
www.twbookmark.com.

An AOL Time Warner Company

Printed in the United States of America

First Printing: March 2002

10 9 8 7 6 5 4 3 2 1

ACKNOWLEDGMENTS

I am grateful to a very large number of people who assisted in developing the information contained in this book. Many of those who contributed do not wish to be named. In any case, it would require several pages to recognize all who assisted.

A few individuals, however, did much to help make this story possible. So a special thanks should go to Linda Stares for translations and explaining Russian customs, George Helland for his insights into Russia and information he provided, Karl Olivecrona for geographical assistance, Margaretha Olivecrona for help with language problems, John Brandon, Owen Osmotherly, and Nick Jones of Oil States MCS for technical information, and Peter Miller, who represented the book.

Several organizations also proved to be helpful. These include Bellona, a diligent and effective group, *The Moscow Times*, *The St. Petersburg Times*, the Russian Naval Museum, *Itar-Tass*, and www.kursk.strana.ru/www.kursk14l.org, vital online news sources.

I also wish to single out Rob McMahon, the editor at Warner Books who had faith in this project and did such a valuable editing job. Thank you, Rob.

And thank you, too, Suzy, for everything.

Clyde Burleson
August 2001

AUTHOR'S NOTE

We live in a communications and information age.

Today, a newsworthy event that holds public attention is covered by the media with an unprecedented thoroughness, as well as a wide divergence of viewpoints.

All this makes it easier than ever before in history to amass a huge number of facts about any gripping incident. The sheer volume of available information, however, makes it difficult to organize it all into a manageable format. And often, that ordering process reveals conflicting reports, which produce more questions than answers.

That was the case in the development of *KURSK DOWN!*

The Internet provided access to daily news sources as well as trade publications in Russia, Europe, England, and the United States. These resources, when properly sorted, delivered an overall picture of the disaster. That same material also produced names and titles of people who were familiar with various aspects of the *Kursk* tragedy. Some of those individuals agreed to discuss the matter over the telephone. Many others did not. Language barriers provided additional stumbling blocks that had to be overcome.

Interviews produced new insights and provided a view beyond published reports. And as information was amassed, translations of official Russian Navy documents took on new meanings. From this vantage point, the structure, contents, and theme of the book became clear.

KURSK DOWN! is more than the recounting of a maritime disaster. It is an adventurous view of a great nation at a crossroads—which makes the story all the more compelling.

KURSK DOWN!

PART I
THE BEAUTY

SHE WAS A BEAUTY. THERE WAS NO OTHER WORD. SHE SAT wide and low in the water, her curving hull a black that absorbed rather than reflected the soft Arctic summer sunlight. She was a leviathan of the deep, made by the hands of man to live under the sea. Here was a dark angel of death, a wreaker of havoc, bringer of war and destruction.

Those who served on her revered her. Some also feared her, because of her power and great size.

Although larger than most ships, submarines are traditionally called boats. This boat was named *K-141* or the *Kursk*—not a graceful title for a lady of her breeding. But the Russian Navy is more practical than poetic. And the city of Kursk, grateful for the honor, has a heroic past.

She'd first been christened Project 949A. Carefully conceived, she was a vastly improved enlargement of an earlier model. *K-141* was one of the biggest nuclear attack submarines in the world.

Her design was radical. She had a double hull. The outer shell, called the superstructure, gave the boat its distinctive oval shape.

Covered with a rubberlike polymer that slicked the surface to add silence and more speed underwater, she had a dark, wet sheen as opposed to the dry look of paint on metal.

Between the superstructure and the inner hull was a space of some 7 to 12 feet. A thousand miles of wiring, hydraulic tubing, piping, and bracing, filled this cavity. Here, too, 24 cruise missiles were stored in their ready-to-launch tubes. Submerged and hiding in the depths, *K-141* could rip-fire a salvo of atomic warheads that doomed targets over 600 miles away.

The inner hull encapsulated the living part of the vessel with crew, controls, and nuclear reactors. Each compartment of the *Kursk* had three or four decks and housed a specific function. Watertight doors separated every section.

The design team planned the double hull to make her a hardier lady. They wanted her to be able to withstand a direct hit by a conventional enemy torpedo or depth charge. To reflect their intent, they dubbed her "unsinkable!"

K-141 was laid down in 1992 at the yards in Severodvinsk, a famed shipbuilding town on the Beloye More or White Sea. Skilled craftsmen cut and shaped each steel plate. Every centimeter of every weld was tested, every joint pressure-checked and x-rayed. Form followed function and beauty emerged. The boat's function was devastation. Therefore, the beauty was tinged with subdued violence.

Launched in 1994, she was almost 500 feet long and nearly 60 feet wide. Lying still, her bottom reached some 30 feet beneath the cold water. The line of her vast curving deck was broken by a large sail or conning tower bearing the proud red and gold symbol of the Russian Navy. Jutting upward from the sail, like shining lances, were slender radio masts, periscopes, and air intakes.

At the rear, her huge rudder reached clear of the water, hinting at the boat's enormous maneuverability.

Submerged, she was home. She could remain down for 120 days, traveling at a speed of 28 knots, and dive to depths approaching 3,000 feet. When running, she hummed and the twin propellers made a distinctive cavitation sound. When hiding, she could lie still and silent, defying detection.

K-141 was the best of her sisters. There was pride in those assigned to the other boats. Those who served on the *Kursk* were reverent. They knew and sensed her superiority. An indescribable feeling ran through her many corridors, compartments, and decks. It was as though the iron that formed her was special—as if she were made of steel from meteorites, the metal fallen to earth after being forged by a journey through space.

While her destructive power might have had many uses in time of war, she was created for one purpose— to hunt and sink aircraft carriers. Hers was a daunting assignment. She had to avoid the protective cordon of ships ringing her prey, slip quietly past opposing submarines, attain a launch position for her torpedoes or missiles, and make her kill.

She had been built for that moment, armed for that moment, her crew trained for that moment. It was her destiny. Or so her creators, and those who served aboard *K-141*, believed.

PART II
THE DISASTER

12 August 2000—1140 Hours (Moscow Time)
On Board Submarine K-141 (Kursk)

The explosion that had ripped through the submarine polluted the air with smoke and the sharp stench of burned electrical insulation. The small group of men who survived had found each other in the aftermath and taken shelter in the massive boat's ninth compartment.

Moving about was difficult because debris covered the steeply slanting metal deck. That was just as well because movement increased their respiration rates. Breathing faster used up their small supply of life-giving air more quickly.

Captain-Lieutenant Dmitry Kolesnikov, in his role as senior officer left alive, had assumed command. Standing six feet three inches tall and weighing over 200 pounds, he exuded a friendly confidence. The combination of a handsome, youthful face, reddish-blond hair, and blue eyes added to his charm. Even though he was young, he was an experienced, competent submariner. He knew their situation was desperate. The others knew it, too.

That understanding must have made his efforts to maintain morale and discipline more difficult.

There was no way to escape. They were trapped on the bottom, 300 feet underwater, surrounded by an icy sea. The escape hatch in their compartment might have been damaged. It made little difference. With no breathing apparatus, chances of making a free ascent to the surface were slim. Even if they did succeed, they had no inflatable life rafts. How long would they last in the freezing water fighting towering waves? A few minutes? A half hour? No more, surely. The Navy was coming to their rescue. What they had to do was remain a team and hold out until help arrived.

Waiting, shivering in the growing cold, each man was alone with his own thoughts and hopes. Help was on the way. It had to be. The Navy would not desert them.

Cut off from the world of warm sunlight and fresh air, a horrid sense of isolation weighed on the group. And beyond question, Dmitry had to have wondered what orders Captain Lyachin would have issued had he been present.

The submarine commander Dmitry so respected wasn't able to help him. Captain Lyachin was dead. The entire crew, except the pitiful few gathered so wretchedly together, were dead, too.

Several of the survivors were seriously injured and their pain must have added to Dmitry's misery. These men were his responsibility. And there was nothing he could do to help them. The small rolls of gauze bandages and tiny bottles of antiseptic in the only first aid kits available were for minor emergencies. They had never been intended to deal with burns and wounds of such serious magnitude.

Repeated intercom calls to the hospital-like sick bay near the crew quarters in Compartment 4 went unanswered. That was not surprising. The blast that had ripped through the submarine originated in a forward portion of the boat.

As senior officer, it was up to Dmitry to provide leadership and bolster the men's spirits. Part of his duties included keeping a record of their plight. Using what paper he could find, he made careful notes. Including himself and his best friend, Rashid, there were 23 survivors. Not many, considering 118 had been on board when they sailed.

He had selected the ninth compartment as headquarters. There was an escape hatch where a DSRV could dock to evacuate them. Despite constant budget cuts, the Northern Fleet still had two of the newer Deep Sea Rescue Vehicles, plus a third older model. So they had hope.

Help would come. He was a member of the most elite group in the Soviet Navy. If he could keep the men acting as a unit and alive long enough, the Navy would rescue them. And he could return to Olga—his Olechka—knowing he'd done his duty. Dmitry and Olga had been married only a few months and she needed him. He needed her, too. Then there was his mother . . . and his dad . . . and his brother.

The dim emergency lighting and deep shadows made numbers on a watch face difficult to read. Had it only been two hours? The question the men must have asked over and over again still remained unanswered. What had happened?

One moment, all had been fine.

The turbines, turned by steam generated with heat

from the pair of nuclear reactors, had been spinning smoothly. A nervous excitement had settled over the crew. The Kursk had been assigned a starring role in the most important part of the annual war games. Making five knots, submerged to a depth of 90 feet, they had been conducting a full combat simulation torpedo run. Captain Lyachin had announced receiving permission for a practice firing.

As commander of the technical party of the main propulsion division, Dmitry was a respected officer and leader of the seventh compartment. On duty, he knew his job and his manner was direct. At 27, he'd managed to pull a lot of undersea time.

His brightly lit workstation had the clean, pungent smell of hot machine oil, accompanied by a hum from the turbines. Gauges and controls were mounted in compact panels on the metal bulkheads. Above them, through neat holes in the steel, bundles of multicolored wiring cascaded down like rainbow horsetails, then vanished again behind a large electronic console.

Captain Lyachin demanded perfection in every maneuver. So the firing run had to be perfect. And to be perfect, Dmitry and his team needed to function as a single unit. All their training, all the hours of meticulous equipment maintenance, had been focused on this one critical task.

The long, hollow, echoing boom, like a distant thunderclap, had been unexpected. Underwater thunder was impossible. That sound must have generated instantaneous jolts of adrenaline that set hearts pounding. Shocked crew members would have seen bulkheads flex and felt the noise rattle deep in their chests. As their boat shuddered, it had lurched nose down, slanting the decks precariously, forcing them to grab anything at hand to remain standing.

When the regulation sequence of short, sharp alarm bells had begun, the strident warning signal was piped throughout the boat.

They had practiced this drill until every man on board reacted instinctively. A crew member had to be at his emergency station before the last bell in the series. That meant half a minute or less. As the lingering echo of the final ring bounced off steel bulkheads, the automatic watertight doors would clang shut. Each compartment was then a sealed entity.

That echoing boom couldn't have been faked. The realization this was not a drill must have been chilling.

Other warning buzzers would have kicked in, creating an unearthly din. But one particular emergency klaxon remained silent. The absence of that single nerve-grating horn indicated all was well inside the nuclear reactors. Whatever was causing their problem wasn't atomic in nature.

Only a minute had passed. Men must have yelled orders as they half ran, half stumbled down corridors. By this point, the smell of burning rubber had started filtering through the round, white ventilation tubes. All sense of time was lost in the confusion.

Suddenly, the floor had leveled out. The captain was very good, and this crew, exceptional—the best in the Northern Fleet. They'd won that distinction during their combat patrol in the Mediterranean Sea. They could deal with an emergency. Many a damaged submarine had been saved by increasing forward speed through the water while surfacing. And this boat had plenty of power.

Dmitry and the men in his compartment must have found a moment of confident hope. They were "atomshiks," nuclear submariners. They had been trained to ignore emotion and respect performance. But whatever relief they held was short-lived—because the world, as they knew it, had ended.

A second explosion shook the boat so violently that no one could have been left standing.

This death stroke came 2 minutes and 15 seconds after the first blowup and was five times larger. Ten times. Twenty times. It had doubled and tripled and quadrupled in destructive force and sheer deadly intensity. It was as if time had been stopped long enough so this eruption was compressed into an instant. The huge submarine was sent skittering like a toy, first one way, then twisting down, then snapping bow up with astonishing force.

Those on board must have known the source of the devastation. It sprang from the bow of the boat—where torpedoes were stored. If it had been the cruise missiles housed alongside the sail, everyone would be dead.

The few still alive had to have been partially deafened from the prolonged noise. Even dulled hearing, though, would have been enough to register the agonized squeal of thick metal plates, shrieking as they were torn apart.

What happened next reduced the number of survivors. A murderous shock wave spread from bow to stern, bursting the welded seams. All items not securely stowed became deadly missiles. Flying tools and equipment killed or maimed, leaving dead and dying behind.

That destructive blast was followed by an even more

terrible enemy. *Incandescent gases from the explosion ignited the air and searing fire shot into every part of the submarine. Flames whooshed at almost sonic speed through the ventilation shafts, erupting from grills and openings, scorching and melting all they touched. The inferno came and was gone in a pulse beat, leaving only devastation. Whole looms of wiring had been torn from their mountings and strewn about. The deck was covered with refuse, broken metal, and trash of all descriptions. The air was hazy and the sting of smoke from electrical fires must have burned in the survivors' lungs. Only military discipline would have kept some of those still alive functioning.*

Then the lights went out. With no warning, they were encapsulated in a stygian darkness. Every sense would have been canceled, leaving those still capable of feelings scared, disoriented, and panting for breath.

CHAPTER 1

10 August 2000—0600 Hours (Two Days Earlier)
K-141 Staff Meeting
Vidyaevo, Russian Federation

CAPTAIN 1ST RANK GENNADI P. LYACHIN WAS AN EXCEP-
tional officer. Respected for his consistently outstanding
performance, he was precise, efficient, and decisive. He
came from the region of Volgograd, an area dominated by
the Volga River. And at the age of 45, he was recognized
as one of the finest submarine commanders in the Russian Navy.

Before departing on any mission, a preembarkation
conference with the boat's officers was a mandatory rit-
ual. The gathering he held before leaving port for the
Northern Fleet maneuvers must have been particularly
tense. The *Kursk* had a reputation as the best submarine
in the fleet. And Captain Lyachin was not known for his
patience with those who shirked any facet of their jobs.

Dmitry Kolesnikov's report had to have been typical. As leader of the seventh compartment, it was his responsibility to describe any deficiencies or irregularities with the turbines. There were no problems. All was in readiness for the inspection and coming sea duty.

Lyachin had held this command for about a year and learned a great deal about the personal lives of his officers and crew. So he knew Dmitry had true potential and was a career man. He was the son of a submariner and his brother had also become a naval officer. He came from solid stock and had been trained at Dzherzhinsky Naval College in St. Petersburg, an exceptional school. Dmitry had the necessary dedication. One day he would make an excellent commander. Lyachin had accepted Dmitry's report. They were facing a major seaworthiness inspection in a few hours. It would have been unthinkable for Dmitry's section not to be fully prepared.

Captain Lyachin must have sensed the nervous excitement of his men. Having to make a formal statement of preparedness to him, in front of fellow officers, strengthened the bond between them. Navy men of this caliber would do anything in their power not to let down their comrades. The *Kursk* would be declared ready for navigation, diving, and deep-sea operations.

In his final hours on shore, Lyachin's spirits had to have been high. He was the most fortunate of men. He was allowed to command the best submarine in the entire Russian Navy, possibly the finest sub in the world. And he was about to demonstrate the quality of his boat, along with the efficiency of his crew. They were to play a major role in the largest northern sea maneuvers in more than a decade.

Over 30 ships and subs, as well as many aircraft, were participating. They would hold mock attacks, fire missiles and torpedoes, and use their latest equipment. To Lyachin, the most important benefit was that his men would get valuable time at sea to further refine their skills. They needed sea duty, but funds were simply not available. At least someone at Fleet HQ had the good sense to recognize that submariners required time underwater to keep their abilities sharp. So his people got more hours offshore than most—not enough, but all the limited budget could afford. Anyway, just participating in this massive exercise was an honor. And winning the top prize could have a positive effect on coming promotions.

The Northern Fleet's sea trials had another huge benefit. The maneuvers would better prepare his crew for their next combat tour of the Mediterranean. Demonstrating Russian naval strength to other nations, both favorable and unfavorable to the new Federation, helped maintain prestige throughout the world. If financing was available, he would favor a year-long showing of the fleet and flag.

Always cautious, Lyachin must have had several concerns before departing. One dealt with the torpedoes. They might be requested to fire one of the damn liquid-propelled fish. If so, he wanted to make certain Senior Lieutenant Aleksey Ivanov-Pavlov, the torpedo officer, understood that special care must be taken. A careful watch had to be posted on those liquid-fueled torpedoes. Such an action probably wasn't necessary, but it was certainly prudent.

The only good in using an unstable liquid propellant was financial. The kerosene/hydrogen peroxide mixture was not as safe as either the solid-propellant weapons or those driven by an electric motor. The Navy high command had argued against using the liquid-fueled models and lost. It must have been hard for Lyachin to justify adding any degree of danger to his boat just because the torpedoes were cheaper than those they were to replace.

It was always the money. Everyone knew the oligarchs had stolen the nation blind. And most funding allocated for military uses went to the Army, to support its futile operations in Chechnya. As usual, the Navy was forced to make do with the leftovers.

Once on board the *Kursk*, Lyachin was in his element. The men he passed would have snapped to attention until he waved them back to their duties. The crew had become accustomed to seeing him in every part of the boat. His unanticipated presence kept them sharp.

The *Kursk* had been commissioned in 1995 and assigned to the 7th SSGN Division of the 1st Submarine Flotilla of the Northern Fleet. Despite six years of hard service, constant maintenance had erased most signs of wear. A polished plaque was fastened to a bulkhead midway along the main corridor. The inscription dedicated the submarine to the city of Kursk. Seven of the crew were from there and formed a tight little group. They kept their plaque shined, too. That sort of camaraderie, built on pride and common loyalty, was one more force that kept the men enthusiastic.

The people of Kursk found a nationalistic spirit in having *K-141* named after their city. They donated welcome amounts of money for the boat's upkeep, items of food, and prayers for their safety. Young men of that region considered it an honor to serve aboard her. Many applied for that duty to meet their mandatory military service requirement. And they did this even though the tour on a submarine was for a minimum of three years as opposed to the normal two-year conscription period.

The submarine so many admired had been laid out by the renowned Igor Spassky and principal designer I. L. Baranov with Rubin Central Design Bureau. The NATO designation for this class of boat was "Oscar II." To a Russian officer, she was of the "Antey" class. Called by any name, *K-141* was one of the deadliest attack submarines in existence.

The *Kursk* was powered by two nuclear reactors that allowed the massive boat to hide in the deep for long periods of time. The pair of giant, seven-bladed screws at the stern assured rapid acceleration in an emergency. And in case of a problem, she could operate on one reactor or the auxiliary diesel engine she carried.

Hours later, after a full day of brass and inspections, Lyachin probably took refuge in one of his favorite places on the boat. The lookout station, housed inside the tall sail, was a good place to be alone. The space featured square portholes that could be dogged closed for weather protection when surfaced.

The view from so high above the deck had to have been stunning. In early evening the light was still bright at such a high latitude. Summer was one of the few benefits of being stationed at Zapadnaya Litsa on the Kola Peninsula. There were several naval towns and Northern Fleet bases in the area, including Vidyaevo, where Lyachin lived with his wife. All the settlements were little more than rural hamlets. If a person wanted culture, it was necessary to go to Murmansk, not so far away.

From the lookout, the hills and trees, which for much of the year were covered with snow, formed a landscape of brown and green. The port's huge cranes, no longer in working order, stood like immense rusting scarecrows against the blue sky. Below, along the piers, gray concrete stretched for miles, defining slips for boats of the flotilla. The subs were kept widely separated for safety considerations.

Activity along the wharves would have been intense, with the unmuffled roar of diesel truck engines loud enough to make conversation difficult. Sea smells of aged iodine and salt that blended with the sulfurous reek of bunker oil permeated the submarine.

By turning slightly, Lyachin would have been facing in the direction of the small apartment where he and Irina lived. Navy life was hard on women. Their men could be gone for months at a time. She was a good wife, though, and another source of his pride.

The premission inspection had gone well. This in spite of noncompliance with the regulation that required every sub returning from a mission to be stripped of its armament. Removal allowed for better inspection of the individual weapons and a more effective check of the onboard facilities for storing them. It also prevented an accidental explosion while docked that might damage port facilities or nearby vessels.

The top Navy officers were in complete agreement with the precaution. But what could they do? The cranes were totally worn-out and useless. Without machinery, unloading the missiles and torpedoes was impossible. Their only recourse was to require frequent onboard checks and rechecks. The issue again was money.

In the sail of the *Kursk*, paint on the bulkheads had been scraped or worn away in places to reveal the dried-blood-colored antirust primer coating. There was not even enough cash to buy paint to maintain appearances.

Later that evening, in compliance with regulations, Lyachin held a final review of their assignment. It was challenging but his crew could do it.

In addition to five captains from 7th Submarine Division Headquarters along as observers, he had also been ordered to accommodate two representatives from Dagdizel, the military arms factory in Dagestan. Both were torpedo design experts and could help with safety measures—unless they were along for another reason. The Navy tended to carry the secrecy of its projects to extremes. In any case, all elements seemed ready and he expected a good cruise.

Dmitry Staroseltsev, a 19-year-old seaman from the city of Kursk, had found a new world aboard *K-141*. He'd completed his studies at the Railway College and faced mandatory military service. His friends had not been surprised when he turned down a slot in the elite Kremlin Guard for submarine duty. Those who knew him were aware of his love for machinery and his dream of serving in the fleet.

Getting assigned to the *Kursk* had not been easy. There had been three applicants for every slot on the boat allotted to conscripts. Inducted in November and shipped off to camp after a blessing from the Bishop of Kursk himself, he survived eight hard months of training. For Dima, as his buddies called him, the effort had been worth it. He'd thrived in the Navy and gained 17 pounds.

His mom, Valentina, a nurse, had feared her gentle son would not do well in military life. His letters had convinced her otherwise.

"Thank God I'm finally here," he wrote.

His reference to God came easily. He had often accompanied his mother and sister, Inna, to the small, bright yellow church near his home. They lived in a one-story brick house on a tree-lined dead-end street and he had fond memories of the place—especially his mother's cooking.

"Everyone, including officers, called one another by their first names and the officers were almost fathers," one letter he'd written while on a cruise said. "We have four meals a day here, just like home. I'm really happy. We will resurface in the middle of August. See you soon."

Life on board the *Kursk* had settled into a routine for Dima. Stationed in the fourth compartment that contained crew quarters and dining facilities, he was a bilge seaman and his duties were not arduous. So there was time to meet with the six other young men from Kursk and share memories of home.

Dima's best friend, Aleksey Nekrasov, known as "Lyosha," a turbine operator in the seventh compartment, was also pleased with his assignment. His section was under the command of Captain-Lieutenant Dmitry Kolesnikov. Their job was to operate and maintain the mighty twin OK-9 turbines that could be harnessed to produce enough electricity to fill the needs of a small city.

All told, a duty tour on board the *Kursk* was satisfying. The men were part of an elite group, buoyed by a powerful esprit de corps that set them apart. And they were ready to prove exactly how good they really were during the fleet maneuvers.

Aboard the Kursk

Total darkness, like that in the deepest cave, had embraced the survivors. The black would have been almost palpable, like a paralyzing blanket that curdled spirits and confused their brains.

The deck had acquired a horrible new and much sharper slant. How long since the explosions? Seconds? Minutes? The only sound was the unmistakable whoosh of compressed air forcing water out of the ballast tanks. That one roaring noise, combined with the impossible deck angle, told them the Kursk was sinking.

Then suddenly, as if the Lord had decreed it, there was light.

Those still alive had to have been momentarily blinded by the brightness. Elation over returned vision, however, was short-lived. A loud, stomach-wrenching jolt caused items that had been thrown down once to be tossed again in every direction. The mighty submarine shook, her steel plates and stanchions making a forlorn howl. Then all was silent, except for dripping water.

Those on board knew she'd slammed nose first into the seabed. They were living the terror of every submariner. The Kursk, their boat, a pride to all, was down.

It must have taken a few moments for the survivors inside the sunken vessel to gather their senses. The devastation around them was disorienting. Then, as the realization of their plight took hold, the answer to one question held their chances for survival.

How deep were they?

Each of them had passed the mandatory submariner test of ascending from an emergency escape hatch to the surface, more than 100 feet above, without any type of breathing apparatus. And the officers on board knew special care had been taken while maneuvering the giant boat because of shallow water in the exercise area.

Determining how deep the submarine rested would reveal their best course of action. But estimating the depth was difficult. The lights could not have been out long before the emergency system cut on. From the instant the deck slanted away and the main electrics had failed, no more than a minute could have passed. It must have seemed infinitely longer, but the battery-powered units would have activated sooner than that.

The boat had twisted and skidded through the water. They couldn't have been going very fast or she'd have busted in the middle—maybe ten or so knots initially, slowly accelerating. And they'd started from a depth of about 90 feet. So, possibly they were down as little as 300 feet. Even with the tail of the boat sticking upward, it was too deep for an unaided escape.

After impact, metal plates forming the smashed hull would have emitted a terrible creaking—an unbearable noise of low groans and high-pitched pings that hurt the ears. Would the pressure hull hold? There was no way to tell. As the boat's shape melded to the sea bottom, the weird shrieks would have diminished.

Dmitry must have forced himself to think. The discipline drilled into him would have dictated his actions. His first task was to report to the Command Center. There was no response over the boat's intercom. The other constantly manned station was the sick bay in the fourth compartment. Nothing there, as well. Either the communications system was busted or . . . It was better not to dwell on the "or" part.

The crew of a submarine is a tight group and, at sea, they live in restricted space. So Dmitry knew the men assigned to each of the compartments in the rear of the boat. His group in Compartment 7 totaled eight, plus himself. The sixth compartment was staffed by five, including his buddy, Rashid Ariapov. Compartment 8 contained seven, and the end of the boat, the ninth compartment, had a crew of three. That made 24. Everyone would have been at his duty station, both because of the simulated combat torpedo attack run and in response to the first emergency alarm that had slammed the watertight doors.

They had no way to judge how seriously their boat was damaged. So some exploration was necessary. At the same time, the remaining crew could be located and sent to muster in the ninth compartment, near the escape hatch. And they could care for any injured men as well.

The inspection of the boat must have been mentally devastating. The fifth compartment watertight door refused to open. That fact, combined with the force of the two separate explosions, clearly indicated the entire front half of the submarine was flooded. From this came the realization they were probably the only ones still alive.

When all were assembled, there was a head count. Including Dmitry, 23 had survived. What had happened to the missing person? There was no use considering all the possibilities.

By retreating to the rear of the vessel, they had placed three more watertight doors between them and the incoming sea. That was not as comforting as it sounded, because there was the distinct possibility they might be taking water in the lower corridor. The propeller drive shaft seals may have failed, too, providing additional leaks. That understanding would have made clear how helpless their situation really was.

Dmitry had been taught trapped men face two self-destructive dangers.

First was the breakdown of the chain of command. Disorganization led to individuals acting on their own as opposed to working as a team. Among other problems, a riot over food or water might occur.

Second was the slow, irreversible withdrawal into hopelessness. If unchecked, the process might lead to insanity.

Dmitry must have dug through the rubble until he found writing materials. The edges of the paper sheets were charred but would do. He needed to make an official report.

What had caused the disaster? Recalling the events in proper time sequence was important. There had been one initial explosion. It had occurred on board or close by in *the water. A fire had followed. Command had been call-ing for fire-suppression teams over the loudspeaker.*

Then there had been the second mother of all blasts. It must have been the torpedoes stored in Compartment 1. A detonation of that intensity would have ruptured the bow area, which would explain their steep descent to the sea bottom. There was little comfort in that explanation. He could recall the roar of ballast tanks being blown. If this indestructible submarine still went under, even with negative ballast, damage was extensive.

What else had happened? No klaxon had announced problems with the nuclear reactors. They apparently had gone into emergency shutdown mode. That fail-safe seemed to have worked. But it left them without power.

Logic dictated their course of action. If they had guessed correctly, the crippled Kursk was not deep. The explosions had to have been detected. Therefore help was on its way and a DSRV could reach them. That was logi-cal, true, and simple. The men would believe it.

The Deep Sea Rescue Vehicles were their best hope. Two trips by even one of the smaller, older model DSRVs would be able to transport the survivors to the surface. What they must do was hold out. The Northern Fleet would come. They had to come, if Dmitry was ever going to see Olechka again.

Slowly the survivors had to have realized it was grow-ing colder. With no electricity there would be no heating. Eventually, the sub would assume the same near freezing temperature as the water surrounding it.

Dmitry Kolesnikov knew maintaining a positive state of mind was a critical challenge. It would be easy to slip into depression. So probably he and the rest of the men sought cheerful memories. Dmitry must have remembered his 27th birthday, two days before.

He'd reported for duty on board the Kursk. They would be 96 hours at sea. That was the good part. Time underwater was becoming more difficult to acquire.

Money had not been such a problem in his father's time. His dad had been a 1st captain on a nuclear submarine—one of the early atomshiks. They had no equipment shortages. The Navy got the best in those days, and the nuclear sub fleet better than that.

His father, Roman, had visited the Kursk. He had been impressed, especially with the spacious crew quarters. Accommodations had been considerably more cramped on those earlier boats.

His father had not pressured him to join the Navy. Being a submariner was a glamorous job. You were respected. Roman had told him he would never get rich on Navy pay and that it was an unhealthy, thankless life. The friends you made, though, would be just that—true friends for the rest of your life.

Dmitry had spent two days in his room, avoiding other people, thinking through what he wanted as a career. The submarines had won. For him, it was almost a religious calling. He would dedicate his life to the Navy. With that decision came a characteristic determination. He was totally committed.

When the medical section of the Navy examining board had decided he was 13 pounds overweight for his height, Dmitry responded immediately. He dieted on cucumbers and yogurt for almost a week, was reexamined, and accepted.

He'd graduated at the top of his class—which was

how he'd been assigned to the Northern Fleet and earned a berth on the Kursk.

Dwelling on pleasant thoughts must have been harder for the men because of the horrid metallic moans made by the sub's bow as it settled deeper into the bottom sludge.

The lights seemed dimmer. They had pulled all the battery packs from the emergency illumination systems in the other compartments and were using as few at a time as possible. Each of them had already sampled the terrible darkness. No one wanted to contemplate what it would be like when the final lamp died.

CHAPTER 2

10 August 2000
Barents Sea—Northern Fleet Maneuvers
Aboard the Kursk

Teams of sailors had worked through the night loading
supplies and performing last-minute chores on *K-141*. By
0500, with the northern sun above the horizon, they were
done. One by one, the necessary forms were checked and
signed. An old Navy joke maintained that while the world
thought Russian subs ran on nuclear power, they were actually fueled by paperwork.

The morning was clear and clean with a promised high
of about 60 degrees. By 0930 hours, all departure preparations on board the *Kursk* were complete. A senior delegation from Northern Fleet HQ had filed down the
gangway and lingered on the dock. Elderly men, wearing
their peaked officer's caps and bundled against the early
morning chill, they carried themselves with pride. Each

had at one time commanded a vessel. Now they were more like diplomats or government managers.

From their comments, Captain Lyachin had learned the maneuvers had taken on a political light. On August 11, the next day, there was to be a high-level conference in the Kremlin to determine future Russian military policy. In a real sense, the meeting would help decide which branches of the armed forces would receive additional funding. From that, the Northern Fleet might obtain much needed financial assistance. A good showing during the exercises was now doubly important.

The admirals' departure produced a more relaxed atmosphere throughout the submarine. Having top brass on board always placed extra strain on the crew. And today, the men did not need any added distractions. Excitement ran through the massive vessel like an electric current. Intent men hurried along the corridors inside the *Kursk*, minds focused on the job at hand. The hull and bulkheads silently vibrated with an energy that transmitted itself to those in every compartment.

Shortly before 1000 hours, a classic order, *"Otdat shvartovy,"* to cast off all lines, was given and they were under way. Deck crews scurried over the polymer-coated steel plates, heavy hawsers splashed into the oily water, and the *Kursk* slowly inched forward, pushed by her twin propellers. The requisite tugboats stood by to assist as required during the short trip down the channel into the sea.

In the seventh compartment, Captain-Lieutenant Dmitry Kolesnikov and his team of eight monitored the turbine speeds. It was a relief to be moving, as opposed to nervously waiting like an expectant father. The sooner they saw action, the better.

Traveling on the surface, the *Kursk* was ponderous and slow to answer to her helm. Only half of her great rudder was submerged and the streamlined shape of her curved belly presented little resistance to the water. So special care had to be taken with every maneuver and each turn in the channel had to be managed with precision.

Captain Lyachin, along with his complement of officers and men, had commanded the boat from stations inside the conning tower high on the sail. After reaching the open ocean, they remained topside until the vessel was well clear of land. When reports from the navigation and depth-finding teams indicated the submarine had attained a safe position, he led them down the maze of ladders and through corridors to the boat's Command and Control Center. Also known as the Combat Command Center, or "CCC," this was the nexus of the boat's operational capabilities. Information from hundreds of sensors was read, interpreted, and fed into the CCC. Orders, based on that data, then flowed out and were executed. This endless process continued minute by minute, around the clock without letup. To satisfy himself all was ready to perform at peak efficiency, Lyachin would have personally verified the latest compartment status reports. The next task was one every person on board had anticipated.

Warning klaxons would have reverberated throughout the vessel. The enormous black shape that had plowed so ponderously through the waves gently slipped under the dark sea. Once fully submerged, the behemoth found a new life.

More than twice as long as a Boeing 747 jumbo jet,

she handled with the agility of a fighter plane. That analogy is fitting, because the *Kursk* was "flown" through the ocean depths using controls much like those on an aircraft. Vertical and horizontal stabilizers, set at the extreme rear of the boat, made the sleek vessel turn, climb, and dive. Gliding at maximum speed, she was capable of maneuvers few other submarines could equal.

In Compartment 1, far forward in the bow, the two Dagdizel experts probably wasted little time before beginning their work. Mamed Gadzhiyev, chief of the Dagdizel torpedo design office at the plant in Kaspiysk, Dagestan, was assisted by his deputy, Senior Lieutenant Arnold Borisov. They had been enthusiastic about sailing with the *Kursk*, as the short cruise would give them an opportunity to test new ideas. Their first project was to fit an improved battery to one of the older electric-powered torpedoes. Hoping for a major performance enhancement, they unpacked their gear.

Loosening screws and unsealing the various panels that needed to be removed for access to the power-supply module took some time. They had no reason to hurry and behaved in their usual secretive fashion. With this pair, security was a way of life. So it was strange that the two men were openly angry when they discovered the special battery they'd brought with them was too large to fit the allotted space.

Despite attempts to keep it quiet, that news must have brought curious looks to many faces as it spread through the boat. Two top engineers, from a factory with such a high reputation, and they didn't know what size to build a battery. More than one finger was rubbed against a nose in a knowing manner. Clearly, that pair was along for something else altogether. And that something else obviously had to do with the liquid-propellant torpedoes. Or perhaps it was a secret weapon. Or maybe it involved a major safety modification to the Shkval-model torpedoes. Theories abounded.

What many knew for certain was that in 1998, the *Kursk* had visited the Sevmash Shipyards in Severodvinsk for alterations to some of its torpedo tubes. The military newspaper, *Red Star*, had even printed a story on this conversion. It was also known on board that for the sea maneuvers, the submarine was carrying three types of torpedoes.

First, there were the model 65-76 long-range antisurface ship units designed in 1976. Torpedoes, when first used on submarines, had been called "tin fish" and the name, in shortened form, "fish," stuck. This 65-76 fish can alter its path through the water, seeking the target it has been deployed to destroy. In case of a miss, it is capable of using its homing sensors in a reattack mode. During a reattack, it recognizes when it has missed its target, turns, and initiates a new assault to deliver a 450-kg warhead. This model is driven by a liquid High Test Peroxide (HTP) system that produces highly volatile and explosive hydrogen gas. The gas drives a turbine that furnishes quiet power to twin screws. Once loosed, the projectile makes excellent speed and has a more than adequate range. Safety tests indicate this torpedo could resist exposure to fire for a little over two minutes before exploding. Two minutes does not give fire suppression teams much time to act before disaster strikes.

The far safer USET-80 weapon, also stored on board,

dated back to 1980. It relies on a silver-magnesium battery that utilizes water to produce electricity. The driving propeller is then turned by an electric motor. While its top speed is under 50 knots, the USET-80 is extremely reliable. Exposed to fire in a combat situation, these can take three times more heat than the 65-76s before exploding. This margin greatly enhances chances for crew survival.

Finally, the *Kursk* was equipped to handle the Shkval-class torpedoes. Shkval means "squall" in English. This weapon, designed in 1977, caused a storm of amazement when its existence became known after the collapse of the old Soviet Union. The Russians had managed to keep the Shkval and its revolutionary technology secret. When fired, a Shkval, which is rocket-propelled, emits a large volume of gas that encapsulates the entire torpedo. This gas bubble drastically reduces friction between the metal of the projectile and the water. Traveling in its envelope, this undersea missile can reach a velocity in excess of 200 miles per hour. Speeding five times faster than any other torpedo in history, the Shkval can strike a target before evasion or countermeasures can be used as defense.

This silver bullet, in its early form with a tactical nuclear warhead, was a kind of suicide weapon. It had three drawbacks. First, it could only travel in a straight line. Second, it had limited homing capabilities. Third and most alarming, its range was a mere ten miles. An underwater atomic explosion, even a small one, can produce a shock wave strong enough to destroy the attacking sub within ten miles of blast center.

An improved Shkval, with a conventional explosive warhead, was tested in the summer of 1998. Still newer prototypes were known to exist.

The Shkval requires special torpedo tubes that must be built to withstand the very high pressures involved during launching. This explains the modifications to the *Kursk* two years earlier. Many Russian sources believe the pair of engineer-designers from Dagdizel, which is located on the Caspian Sea and manufactures Shkval's propulsion system, were present to test new modifications to the Shkval.

Rumors about some type of secret weapon on board the *Kursk* abounded long before the boat sailed. On honest review, these stories seem dubious. The Russian Northern Fleet Command was well aware that its at-sea war games would be extensively monitored by U.S. satellites, surface electronic surveillance ships, and submarines. English and NATO forces would also have "eyes" on the activity. Testing a revolutionary, highly classified weapon under such scrutiny would be self-defeating.

Cruising at a comfortable 20-plus knots just below periscope depth, the *Kursk*, following regulations, trailed a long-range radio antenna, monitoring on-air traffic between ships of the maneuver flotilla. Communications links by satellite also connected the sub with Northern Fleet HQ and the operation flagship, the Heavy Nuclear Missile Cruiser *Pyotr Velikiy (Peter the Great)*.

Captain Lyachin had been briefed on procedures to be used during the exercise. He, in turn, had made certain the appropriate officers on his staff completely understood all directives that would be in effect.

During the sea exercises, only dummy warheads would be used. Despite this, there was still a considerable degree of danger. All military combat training activities were hazardous because they involved weapons specifically designed to kill, maim, and destroy. Even the simplest exercise was like juggling bottles of nitroglycerin. One careless mistake could cause a lot of harm.

To alleviate at least some of the risk, an intense level of planning had been done by the Northern Fleet staff. Strict rules, along with elaborate checks and balances, were created. These regulations determined where individual vessels would be, timing for all missile launches or torpedo firings, direction of a launch, and other protective issues. No deviation from orders would be permitted. The safety of every submarine, plane, and ship in the operation rested on strict compliance with these mandates.

Operational zones had been established for each of the 30-odd vessels that were to play various roles in the games. In addition, flyways, as well as air-restricted areas, had been established to keep helicopters and planes out of each other's paths.

In short, every precaution in keeping with a hazardous military exercise had been taken. If all participants played exactly by the rules, and, as always the case in these matters, there was a little luck, there would be no casualties.

The *Kursk* had been assigned a 15-by-20-mile patrol area. This 300-square-mile strip of open ocean had a fairly constant depth of about 350 feet. Relative to the sub's length of just over 500 feet, this meant great care had to be taken in terms of violent dives or quick vertical movements. With that understood, lack of deeper water presented no real handicap to the boat's freedom of operations.

In addition to other tasks, the *Kursk* had two main responsibilities. The next day, on Friday, August 11, her crew was to launch one of her Granit-type cruise missiles at a naval target. A direct hit would gain the boat high marks. Their second and much more difficult challenge would come on Saturday, August 12. Working inside specific time limits, the *Kursk*, along with other submarines involved in the training program, would carry out a torpedo attack on a fleet of combat ships acting as the "aggressor" or "opponent." The cruiser, *Peter the Great*, would assume the role of an aircraft carrier and be the primary target. Reports indicate two or more of the Shkval units had been modified for practice firings by removing their warheads. Other sources maintain that the Shkvals had improved propulsion systems that were still experimental.

As the *Kursk* arrived on station, detailed accounts note that Captain Lyachin made the necessary radio calls to verify he was in his assigned patrol zone. His officers would have continued repetitive training sessions to improve missile-launching skills, and each system on the boat would have been checked for readiness. All considered, it was a long night for the crew. And the next day had every promise of being even more hectic.

11 August 2000 —1155 Hours

Submariners in every Navy face a dilemma. They practice endlessly for battle. Yet the only instance in history of a nuclear-powered submarine actually attacking an enemy vessel occurred in 1982. A British boat, the HMS *Conqueror*, followed the Argentine cruiser, *General Belgrano*, for 48 hours during the brief Falkland Islands dispute between those two nations. The *Conqueror* fired a shot and sank the *Belgrano*.

So if history was a reliable indicator of the future, training to fight was probably as close as the crew of the *Kursk* would get to using their vessel for combat. God willing, they would never have to go to war. If matters came to that, however, they were known as the ones most likely to do it right.

Hitting a moving target several hundred miles away with a missile fired from a submarine running underwater is a challenge. To accomplish this precision feat, two requirements are mandatory. The weapons officer on the sub must know his exact geographic position, speed, and direction of travel at the moment the missile leaves its launch tube. And second, that same information is required for the target. Missiles can and do use radar and other devices to "home" on their intended victims. These systems, however, are defeated if the missile is not in reasonable proximity of its target.

For decades, American subs could fire when submerged, while Soviet boats had to surface before shooting. It was necessary for the Russians to bring the launch tubes out of the water and take a final electronic fix to pinpoint positions. This deficiency was corrected some years ago. So the *Kursk* was fully capable of loosing a full salvo of its 24 Shipwreck cruise missiles while remaining hidden in the depths.

Prior to scheduled launch time, Captain Lyachin, following exercise orders, is known to have radioed Fleet

HQ requesting permission to make the scheduled test launching. The response, *"Dobro"* (Good), gave him the required clearance to proceed. At 1235 hours, the crew reported being ready for the shoot.

At 1236 hours, Captain 3rd Rank Andrey Silogava, missile officer, and Senior Lieutenant Boris Geletin, launch party commander, according to regulations, had to confirm two separate go codes and unlock the firing guard. Following an exact sequence at 1238 hours, a series of switches, one after another, was clicked on. The missile came alive, the control panel was hot, and the men in the Combat Command Center were on full alert. At 1239, commitment was made to the last electronic position plots. These were fed into the missile's logic circuits. Based on the dictated Northern Fleet time schedule for the actual missile shoot, Lyachin gave the go for launch at 1240. This final command opened the 23-foot hatch that covered a pair of missile tubes.

Blown from the tube by gas, the slender, finned projectile was propelled upward to the surface. Once free of the water, a solid-propellant boost rocket ignited, creating a maelstrom of fire.

"Pusk!" (Shot away!) was the coded signal passed from Lyachin to the *Kursk*'s communications section and on to Northern Fleet Command.

The missile accelerated, thrusting itself into the sky. Higher and higher it climbed, passing 10,000 feet, 20,000 feet, then roaring through the 30,000-foot marker. At 50,000 feet, the steep climb began to level off. Approaching an altitude of 60,000 feet, the rocket fuel had been consumed and the engine died. This automatically shifted propulsion modes. Its KR-93 turbojet engine sputtered into life with a roar louder than a freight train.

The digital inertial guidance system bled in course corrections, and traveling at supersonic speed, the missile hurled itself toward its preselected target. Final course corrections were received from a manned aircraft as planned, and with one deadly last shriek, the ram-jet engine quit. The weapon, now in a prescribed free-fall path, homed on the target from a high angle.

To more accurately simulate a vessel the size of an aircraft carrier, the small target ship sported a number of dish antennas. These gave the missile's radar guidance system an electronic readout like that coming from a much larger ship. The dummy warhead contained sufficient explosive force to allow observers to determine the exact strike point—if it hit home.

Aboard the *Kursk*, more than a hundred miles away, there had to have been relief over a perfect launch and wide-eyed, world-class worry because much could still go wrong. Improper coordinates might have been entered or their position might have been incorrectly calculated. Hell, the damn thing could even ingest a bird on the way up, blocking the ram-jet's air intake.

Missile Officer Captain 3rd Rank Andrey Silogava's job required him to call time hacks, announcing seconds until impact. The pride, personal satisfaction, and reputation of the entire submarine rested on this single shot. So much had been done right, exactly by the book. Yet so much could go wrong in the next few heartbeats.

The missile officer ended his count. *"Popadenie!"* (Impact now!)

Seconds ticked away. A helicopter, zooming in from

the safety zone, would be flying at full throttle toward the derelict target ship to assess damage.

In the third compartment, a radio crackled and announced *"Tsel' porazhena!"* (Strike!)

The signal officer, Captain 3rd Rank Andrey Rudakov, would have instantly relayed the news to the Command Center.

That quick message had to have broken the tension. They'd done well. The best boat, and the best crew, had once again proven their worth.

After accepting brief congratulations from the five Northern Fleet HQ observers, Captain Lyachin would have spoken a few quiet words of praise to the missile party.

Always the commander, the captain was forced to think ahead. The next responsibility would go to Senior-Lieutenant Aleksey Ivanov-Pavlov, the torpedo officer. They had a difficult hide-and-seek game tomorrow and were to shoot one fish.

The sea-games flagship, *Peter the Great*, was to use standard NATO tactics and duplicate the movements of a carrier task force. Surrounded by support vessels and employing its own powerful sonar as well as other electronic countermeasure devices, the cruiser would be a difficult target—especially against an attack run with a single torpedo limit. Captain Lyachin wanted the kill. It was going to be tough and would require perfect timing. His crew was capable of that, and more.

The single worrisome note was the selection of torpedo to be used. The presence of the Dagdizel weapons plant team and the dummy practice warhead to be fitted indicated they might be called upon to fire the ultra-high-speed Shkval. And if that were the case, there was no room for even the slightest hesitation or error. When the firing command was given, that weapon would sit for an instant inside the torpedo launch tube. This interval allowed time to generate the gas for the bubble that gave the fish its extreme high speed. As that gas was produced, pressure in the special launch tube would immediately increase to dangerous levels. If the shot went perfectly, that gas was released harmlessly into the water. If anything went wrong, or firing procedures fell seconds behind, pressures could increase to the point where the tube would rupture, releasing the gases and intense heat into the boat.

Since they'd been unable to remove their armament after the last cruise, the *Kursk* carried her full arsenal of explosive weaponry. It was a dangerous load for war games.

Aboard the Kursk

Four hours had passed since the explosions. There was no question now that they were the only survivors.

A dull lethargy had overcome some of the men. Activity would help break this affliction. Activity would also use their breathable air faster. And the group knew oxygen was their main obstacle to survival. The limited food, water, and lighting could be stretched. When the last of the oxygen in the air was exhausted, though, they were done.

The sea was still seeping into the boat. Every man was aware of this because occasionally a trapped air bubble on one of the decks below squealed like a live creature. It was squeezed by rising water until forced whistling out through small apertures in seams broken by the sub's impact. The same cold, incoming water was also chilling the boat. All metal surfaces inside the sub were coated with droplets of condensation.

The moaning and crying from those who were injured had finally quieted. Talk was less frequent. Conserving oxygen left every man alone with his thoughts. The resulting silence allowed them to hear the ceaseless drip and gurgling sounds of flowing water.

Dmitry took his pencil and paper and began a solemn roll call. In his careful hand, he wrote the name of every man in the group. Next to each, he marked a small, neat cross to indicate that person was still alive.

There was little left for them to do except wait. The Navy would come. Would they be in time? That was the question. The survivors must have believed every passing second brought help closer. And carried them nearer the end.

CHAPTER 3

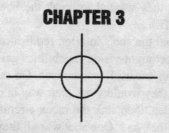

12 August 00—0240 Hours
Northern Fleet Exercise

ON THE BARENTS SEA, A SUMMER SUN OFTEN SHINES AT midnight, sparkling the waves with liquid silver. The long days may be pleasantly mild, with cloudless skies, temperatures in the mid-60s, and gentle swells. As mariners know, the weather can switch from tranquil to turbulent with little warning. So a continuous storm watch played a vital role in the Northern Fleet maneuvers. All participating vessels monitored the reports.

Surface conditions were of little concern to those aboard the *Kursk*. Cruising in her designated patrol area at a depth of 90 feet, the sub glided silently through untroubled waters.

On board, despite the late hour, activity in Compartment 1 must have continued at an urgent pace. The successful missile launch had placed added stress on the torpedo crew. Their need for a model torpedo shot was intense. Working under the precise instructions of the Dagdizel engineers, the team had used the automated-handling equipment to load and unload one of the torpedo tubes with the required practice ordnance. When the attack run commenced and they were given the order to make ready, they wanted to break the boat's record for launching a fish.

Throughout the sub's interior, reddish-orange lighting used to protect night-vision capabilities gave instruments and people an unearthly appearance. On this day, before 1800 hours, they would work their way in close, running silent and deep, then sink the mock aircraft carrier. One shot was all they had. One shot was all they would need. The *Kursk* was going to be the sub that made the kill.

0800 Hours—Aboard the Pyotr Velikiy

Fifty miles from *K-141*'s patrol zone, the *Peter the Great*, fleet flagship for the exercises, progressed full throttle at 30 knots. The day was clear, and a turbulent wake churned by the cruiser's twin screws left foaming white streaks through the blue water. As the sleek vessel began a turn to port, her escort ships changed course accordingly, altering positions to maintain their tight, protective screen. Executed with the precision of a close-order drill team, the flagship's convoy created a naval ballet that blended graceful, coordinated motion with raw energy.

First laid down in Baltic Yard 189, St. Petersburg, in April 1986, the cruiser was launched three years later in 1989 and named the *Yuri Andropov*. Political tides and times saw her rechristened *Peter the Great*. At 826 feet long and only 93 feet wide at the beam, she is a narrow, slender vessel. The first nuclear Russian surface warship, *Peter the Great* utilizes an odd auxiliary oil-fueled system to superheat steam from the reactors to produce added propulsion. In an emergency reactor shutdown, the vessel could continue to maneuver, using this secondary, nonatomic power resource.

Before construction on this ship was complete, work was stopped because of funding shortages. A presidential order was required in order to complete the vessel in time for the 300th anniversary of the Russian Navy.

Normal ship's complement is 82 officers, 644 seamen, and 18 aircrew members. For this exercise, an additional number of high ranking observers were present.

Designed to strike carriers, other surface vessels, submarines, and aircraft, this Kirov-class battle cruiser was fitted with a massive variety of missiles, guns, torpedoes, antisubmarine mortars, and electronic countermeasures. As an added feature, she could also hit targets out of sight over the horizon by using satellite controls for her Shipwreck missiles. These rockets could be launched in salvo or, as the Russians say, rip-fired, one shot right after another. A lead missile would climb to a high altitude and serve as a target spotter. It electronically exchanged information with the others, which flew in a pack only a few feet above the waves. If the pathfinder missile was destroyed, one of the others could be directed to take its place.

The *Peter the Great* also housed three Ka-27 Helix helicopters for surveillance, weapons delivery, and supplemental missile guidance activities.

Standing in the cruiser's bridge, officers could feel the

steel deck vibrate as they completed their turn and began an arc in the opposite direction. Use of a zigzag course was standard procedure for a fleet in enemy-infested waters. It was too early for the mock sub attack, but even so, full protective measures were being practiced.

The Northern Fleet commander, Admiral Vyacheslav Popov, watched the activity intently. His service career had begun in 1971 at a remote station. During the next 29 years, he completed 25 long-range cruises and spent 96 months in the submarine service. In January 1999, a presidential decree advanced him from Navy chief of staff to leadership of the Northern Fleet.

A barrel-chested, muscular, round-faced man with a full head of dark reddish hair, Popov wore a sharply creased summer uniform shirt with shoulder boards to designate his rank. He smoked cigarettes using a holder.

The flotilla should have given him a sense of satisfaction. The exercises were going well—especially the *Kursk*'s missile launch. Lyachin had been precisely on time with his shot and scored a devastating hit on the target.

Popov had personally seen the enthusiasm generated among his officers and men by the war games. Admittedly, the maneuvers were straining the budget, but the expense was worth it. These simulated military operations were particularly important with the talks in Moscow continuing. An excellent showing in the final hours of the effort would go far to help the Navy's position.

Admiral Popov was inspired by the loyalty of his men. In spite of missing paydays and enduring adversities too numerous to mention, they stayed in the service. And somehow, they maintained their proficiency. That took dedication—which was another point to make in Moscow. His Northern Fleet could be the finest Navy in history. The desire was there, the will was there. Only the funding was missing.

While a man of his rank did not take sides, he must have wished the *Kursk* luck in her final hunt. Demonstrating the ability to defend an aircraft carrier against a determined submarine attack was fine. However, Russia only had one carrier on active service. With operating expenses for a carrier so high, it was a miracle they still had one afloat. The Navy did have submarines, though. So a successful sub attack on the carrier was, politically, a far better outcome.

A submarine sinking a carrier would show that the Russian Navy was capable of protecting the homeland. More, it would demonstrate that carriers were not as vital to modern naval warfare as most believed. If, that is, the enemy was confronted with vessels as deadly as the *Kursk*. The ability to nullify the usefulness of the West's aircraft-carrier-based fleets was a blow struck at the heart of their tactics.

It would be unfair to aid Captain Lyachin in some way. Lyachin was a highly capable man and needed no assistance. Even so, one could hope for the most beneficial outcome.

By rules of the simulated war games, Captain Vladimir Kasatonov and the crew of the *Peter the Great* would consider themselves in hostile seas and under potential attack from 1130 hours to 1800 hours. At the end of that time frame, all precautions would be dropped and they would stand down, with the exercise completed.

The *Kursk*, as an additional safety measure, would then depart her defined attack area, break radio silence, and report to Fleet Command.

The procedure was straightforward. The *Kursk* was not to leave its perimeter during the operation and could not attack until the *Peter the Great* entered the prescribed zone.

If everyone followed the rules, the program was safe. Still, as any military man knew, there were dangers in coordinating huge submarines and ships in close proximity.

To make matters worse, American, NATO, and Norwegian vessels were also operating in the area. The Russians maintained a running tally of all foreign assets deployed for observing their activities. The result clearly demonstrated the interest other nations were taking in the Russian games. The U.S. had two subs, the USS *Toledo* and the USS *Memphis*, working near the maneuvers. And there was a U.S. TAGOS electronic surveillance ship, USNS *Loyal*, gathering underwater acoustical data, about 200 miles away. A Norwegian research vessel, the *Marjata*, also in the hunt, had similar capabilities. Finally, they had traced the British submarine, the HMS *Splendid*, as well. Five spies on and under the water plus more eyes in space and a sea floor dotted with hydrophones to catch their every move. That degree of attention was irritating. Then again, if the *Kursk*'s attack was successful, it would certainly be a demonstration of Russian submarine capability.

The most critical part of the exercise would start in a matter of hours. As an experienced submariner Admiral Popov could easily have pictured the activity inside the *Kursk*. Concentration. That was the watchword. The crew needed to focus attention on every detail, especially in the first compartment torpedo room. The tin fish were dangerous.

0848 Hours—Aboard the Kursk

In the Combat Control Center, Captain Lyachin would have been busy, taking reports from his many section chiefs. In just a few minutes he had to meet the requirements of the maneuvers orders by making a mandatory position and status report. At 0851, the *Kursk* contacted the onshore Northern Fleet Operations Center. After providing the necessary information, Lyachin formally requested permission to load and fire a training torpedo. The reply from the Ops Center was again *"Dobro!"*

Armed with this permission, the crew had two and a half hours before the 1130 start time for the exercise. While the torpedo room party made final preparations, Lyachin directed the sub to patrol his assigned 300-square-mile area. He ordered the *Kursk* south, to the extreme edge of his sector, as a navigation proficiency problem. Running in combat patrol mode, the boat then turned to the northwest. On this leg, the vessel slowed to a speed of about eight knots, ran as silently as possible, and ascended to a depth of 60 feet.

After extending the periscope, Lyachin must have ordered the radio antennas for communications as well as their satellite global positioning system raised. And as an added precaution, he utilized the snorkel air intake to fill their high-pressure air tanks. If they had to surface fast, compressed air could instantly be shot from these reservoirs into the water ballast tanks. The "blow" would eject tons of water in seconds, giving the mighty sub greater buoyancy and popping her to the surface. With those preparations complete, Lyachin held course. Next, he posted a visual watch to spot their targets, which at this point were moving toward the designated war zone.

1058 Hours—Aboard the Peter the Great

The *Kursk*'s request to Northern Fleet HQ to load and fire a torpedo had been quickly relayed to Admiral Popov and his group. The "enemy carrier" understood. Captain Lyachin was moving the *K-141* into an attack mode.

With the mock combat about to begin, a *"Vse po mes-tam!"* (battle stations!) signal was given. This set full-alert scanning of all radar, sonar, and other electronic submarine-detection devices into motion. Designed with submarine hunting as part of its total mission package, the cruiser was well equipped for that purpose. Her position, still some 30 miles from the engagement zone, meant she was over-the-horizon from the *Kursk*. So they had no visual contact with the now-hostile sub.

As part of the antisubmarine warfare activity, missiles were readied for launch. And the flotilla of ships surrounding the *Peter the Great* tightened their defensive screen. Actual firing could take place at specified times.

Admiral Popov, according to reports, was annoyed by the incessant NATO, British, and American scrutiny of their activities. Especially bothersome was the daily presence of a Norwegian Lockheed Martin P-3C Orion air-sea patrol plane. As the spies were in international waters, there was little the Russians could do about this intrusion into their operations. A few were probably tempted to try one of their new Anti-Sub Warfare Vodopad missiles on the Americans. A near miss, perhaps? Just to show them their positions were known?

1103 Hours—Aboard the USNS Loyal

In addition to using its full array of onboard sonar gear for monitoring Russian activity, the *Loyal*'s crew had expanded their ship's capabilities. Besides a towed array of underwater detection devices, they had released free-floating sensors that enhanced their information-gathering/processing techniques. After two days of intense activity, technicians on board were functioning at peak efficiency. Keeping a respectable distance from the action, they were intercepting all manner of radio communications.

1104 Hours—Aboard the USS Memphis

Following standing orders, the *Memphis* had taken station for a regular duty tour in the Barents Sea. As a matter of course, the United States maintains two submarines in this area year round. For the war games, a third submarine, the British *Splendid*, had been brought in to perform added reconnaissance duties.

Having so many Russian vessels together in a relatively small zone offered an irresistible intelligence opportunity. One of the most useful surveillance sources for submarines is a library of digitally recorded sounds of individual ships and undersea boats moving through the water. The noise from a given vessel is unique to that vessel. So each electronic "fingerprint" can be automatically accessed and matched against real-time incoming sonar data. These data profiles allow accurate identification, which, in turn, provides information on the combat capabilities of the ship or submarine in question.

During the *Kursk*'s Mediterranean cruise, her distinctive sound pattern had been captured. This allowed operators on the *Memphis* to single her out from background disturbances and readings from other boats. Trailing the *Kursk* from a safe distance became a relatively simple matter.

One submarine tailing another while underwater is a dangerous game. According to Russian reports, during the years between 1967 and 2000, there were 11 documented collisions between Russian subs and those of other nations. Eight of those incidents took place in Northern Fleet test areas. The most recent accidents occurred in the early 1990s. The USS *Baton Rouge*, a Los Angeles-class boat, crashed with a Russian Sierra-2-type boat in February 1992. Both subs were severely damaged. Then in March 1993, the USS *Greyling* collided with a Russian Delta-3 class. Again, both suffered significant damage.

In order to prevent such incidents, and to keep U.S. submarines out of the Russian firing ranges, parameters had been established for proximity to other vessels. These mandated a safe margin of distance while still allowing for continuous observation.

1105 Hours—Aboard the Kursk

The practice torpedoes were in their loading racks and one would be transferred into its tube and made ready to shoot when directed. The captain had to be mentally focused on the tactics and countertactics of the mock attack. Like the rest of the crew, he undoubtedly craved action. Orders were orders, though, so for a while longer it was a waiting game. And waiting was hard.

Visual and electronic scans of the assigned sector still indicated no sign of the *Peter the Great* and her protective cordon of ships. Yet all on board the *Kursk* knew they were coming and what a reception they were going to get.

1109 Hours—Aboard the Peter the Great

Prepping a missile before a shoot is a complex procedure involving three separate teams. The launch party conducts the actual liftoff. While the projectile is in flight, the control party directs its attitude, altitude, speed, and path through the air. The target designation party has the responsibility for precisely defining where the warhead should strike. Bringing all these elements together takes time. If a single person involved in the process is even a little out of practice, the entire operation is drastically slowed. Rehearsal on dry land with simulators is not a strong substitute for performing the tasks on a moving, rocking ship. And sea time had been cut.

Due to this handicap and other equipment difficulties, the missile parties, by some reports, took longer than anticipated to set up their shots. So they found themselves in a serious situation.

Operations orders contained a specific time schedule. They were now an hour past the stated deadline. No one wanted to say why they were behind. And no one was eager to take the blame.

Being late for launching was especially troubling because the delay occurred on the operation's flagship. Worse, it happened while the Northern Fleet commander was on board. If at all possible, the missile launch had to be completed. Fear of repercussions for not firing could have become stronger than the need to follow the exacting exercise time schedule.

1120 Hours—Aboard the Kursk

The real game of undersea stalking and evasion began the instant a sonar operator on the *Kursk* reported being pinged by the fleet's massive sonar sweep. This first detection triggered a counteraction to determine the location of the vessel originating the ping. Within seconds, hunter and hunted knew each other's positions. Moving through the pitch-black sea at a depth of 90 feet, the *Kursk* immediately took evasive action. The submarine swung onto a course that would take them away from the approaching flotilla. Staying within the boundary of their assigned patrol sector, they slipped toward the zone's western edge. The idea must have been to disengage, run, hide, and then attack from a new direction.

Captain Lyachin must have decided that he wanted to intercept the *Peter the Great* at the earliest time allowed by the rules of the exercise. If all went well, he would shoot his torpedo just moments after the approved 1130 engagement hour. The apparent strategy was to attack quickly to surprise their opponent.

It was now imperative the *Kursk* remain undetected. Rigged for silent running, the submarine came to an almost full stop, holding at 90 feet below the surface. Lyachin maintained only enough momentum to give them seaway to maneuver in the slow current. He then ordered ballast adjustments to keep them exactly level in the water, and they waited.

1127 Hours—Aboard the Peter the Great

Reports indicate that in spite of the standing operations orders, commands were issued, and firing sequences for three missiles were started. With an ear-straining roar, the first Vodopad-type weapon blazed into the air, leaving behind a white cloud of smoke and steam. Then one more, tail spouting red flame, punched through the remnants of the earlier launch and disappeared into the deep blue sky.

The third missile, also equipped with an antisubmarine-warfare exploding head that would allow it to seek out a target lying submerged at a shallow depth, was released moments later.

Later comments claim that Captain 1st Rank Sergey Ovcharenko and his associates followed the path of the last Vodopad and watched it drop into the sea.

1127 Hours—Aboard the Kursk

An emergency warning klaxon, reverberating like an electronic car alarm gone berserk, was the first sign of a problem. Shocked, those in the Command Center must have been frozen in place as the first compartment torpedo section leader's voice came yelling over the intercom.

One of the liquid propellant torpedoes was leaking. Everyone instantly understood the danger. There was no time to think. Trained action was required. The faulty weapon had to be loaded into a tube. While this was being done, Lyachin reportedly requested immediate radio contact with Northern Fleet HQ. Russian Navy rules called for jettisoning the torpedo as quickly as possible. This one, however, was probably no practice weapon. It was a live combat model and the *Kursk* was in relatively close proximity to other fleet vessels.

With the connection to headquarters made, the captain asked permission to shoot the torpedo and repeated coordinates for a direction he believed safe. The radio contact lasted only a few seconds. With fleet okay, he gave the order to fire.

1128 Hours

The long silver body of the Vodopad missile screamed skyward. It had been programed to fly a short trajectory. Its onboard sensors detected nothing, so it had no target. It had been fed no target information. Therefore its circuits were neutral. One particularly clever solid-state bundle of transistors and diodes was mindlessly performing its task, searching for radio transmissions. There was no sound as the invisible feelers radiated from the small antenna and then returned, bearing an unusual signal. At the speed of light, dormant commands may have awakened the system's homing capabilities.

The *Kursk*'s short break of radio silence, created by an onboard emergency and coming at a time after the deadline for weapon launching had passed, could have attracted the missile's mindless interest. The submarine lay at the end of an electronic guideway. An explosive dagger was aimed at her heart.

1128 Hours—Aboard the Peter the Great

According to published quotes, Captain Ovcharenko watched the third missile plunge into the sea. Then, to his astonishment, there was a massive, violent explosion. A huge column of water spewed skyward, creating a small mushroom cloud of steam and mist he described as reminiscent of a nuclear blast.

Since all eyes on board the fleet ship had been tracking the missile flights, there was every likelihood Admiral Popov and many of his staff members saw the same powerful undersea cataclysm.

One of the missiles had hit something. An American sub?

Speculation continued as, moments later, according to a published source, a helicopter carrying Admiral Popov lifted from the deck in a whirlwind of deafening noise. Its destination was believed to be Northern Fleet HQ. Other news sources noted than Popov also ordered radio silence for all vessels in the area.

1128 Hours—Aboard the Kursk

In the first compartment, the torpedo crew had to have worked as fast as they were able to lift the leaking weapon carefully into a loading cradle. Next, the fish would have been shifted into a tube and the order to fire given as soon as possible. Once the tube loading door was slammed and locked, a hand would have struck the launch trigger button. There would be a quick vibration as ignition was initiated. Then the torpedo would have been launched.

One of three scenarios was now played out. Or, perhaps more than one came to pass.

In the first, the missile from the *Peter the Great* struck the *Kursk*. An expert, Captain 2nd Rank Vyacheslav Lohmatov, is quoted in a document saying, "Only a missile could have rammed the submarine." This position is backed by a translation of a Northern Fleet report that states a two-by-three-meter hole in the *Kursk*'s hull had its edges curled inside the boat. Metal bent inward indicates a penetration of the hull from the outside.

A second position has the missile dropping into the water close to the *Kursk*. The resulting explosion jolted the sub, shaking a torpedo from its storage rack, causing it to leak.

In the third possibility, highly explosive hydrogen gas from the leaking torpedo filled the confined space in the firing tube. When the order to fire was given, ignition of the propellant, used to shoot the fish out of the tube and into the ocean, lit the gas. With the explosive force of a truck full of nitroglycerin, the weapon exploded.

It is also believable that a fire from the missile impact ignited the hydrogen produced by the leaking torpedo fuel. In any case, the result was the same. Confined by the strong, solid walls of the torpedo tube, the explosive force blew out both ends, destroying the tube cover on the outer hull and, at the same time, demolishing the loading door. This opening allowed a gout of devastating chemical energy into the compartment. The hot gas, heated to a temperature that would melt steel, followed nature's law and expanded to fill the available space. The men there died instantly. Any object or material that could burn, burst into flames. Contained by the water-tight door closing the compartment from the rest of the ship, the fire was held in the torpedo room.

Simultaneously a second tragedy occurred with almost the same speed. Through a hole in the hull produced by the missile, or from the blown open torpedo tube, a solid column of water under pressure shot into the compartment. As water fell onto the deck, it drained downward through emergency vents into the space underneath. Unfortunately, the water did little to quench the raging fire. And in the space below, which had also been holed by the missile or torpedo explosion, more seawater was pouring in. The level quickly rose until automatic bladders, designed to seal off the flooded area, activated themselves, preventing this source of water from extinguishing the flames.

In the Command Center, the men were too well trained and disciplined to panic. The Emergency Stations Alarm would have been sounded. Damage Control division personnel would have raced into the area to assess the situation and suppress fires even though they were hampered by the flooding.

The weight of the incoming water forced the *Kursk*'s bow downward. To counteract this momentum, and following standard emergency procedures, Captain Lyachin should have called for an increase in forward speed and an emergency ballast release. This action would pop them to the surface with enough force to bring the submarine half out of the water like a leaping whale. Because other ships were known to be about, a visual periscope scan was now mandated. At the same time, the sonar team, using their passive system, would have reported all clear, with no sounds around them. Both inspections completed, the captain appears to have given the command.

The huge tanks of compressed air were instantly vented into the ballast containers, forcing tons of seawater out of the submarine and back into the ocean. Lightened, the *Kursk*'s nose swung upward, toward the safety of sky and air.

Aboard the Kursk

For some of the trapped men, deep sleep had become difficult. Heads stuffy from the tainted air and temples throbbing, they would have dozed fitfully. The silence was broken only by the drip of water. Had they been there a day? More? Watch dials showed the passage of hours but time didn't have the same meaning as before. One belief sustained them. Help was on the way. The Navy would not fail them.

CHAPTER 4

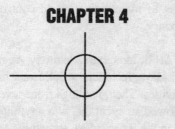

12 August 2000—1129 Hours
NORSAR Observatory, Kjeller, Norway

THE VILLAGE OF KJELLER IS LOCATED IN THE ROLLING
countryside a few miles outside the capital city of Oslo,
Norway. Once a small farming community, the town has
become a center of modern technology. A low, unimpos-
ing building at number 33 Granaveien Street is notable
only because of the array of dish antennas adorning the
roof, hinting at serious communications capabilities.
There is nothing else to suggest that the organization
housed in this facility, which looks more like a factory
than an office complex, has gained worldwide acclaim.
Called NORSAR, it is a private foundation specializing
in seismology and applied geophysics. Founded in 1968
by an agreement between the United States and Norway,
the operation functions at the cutting edge of earth sciences. Using seven strategically placed sensing array
stations, NORSAR is one of the largest seismological ob-

servatories in existence. Through computers and other electronic assistance, NORSAR maintains a ceaseless watch for all forms of seismic disturbances. It can even identify vibrations from underground testing of nuclear weapons. These capabilities make the organization a valuable asset in maintaining world control of military atomic weaponry.

At NORSAR headquarters, Saturday, August 12, began as a normal day. Technicians followed their ordinary morning activities. Then, readings from several of the instruments showed an event that was anything but routine. At 11:28:27, in the Barents Sea, something had happened. And that phenomenon caused a reading of 1.5 on the Richter scale. Almost before the scientists could react to this anomaly, a second event occurred. That incident was so violent the tracing turned into a solid black smudge. The location was identical to the earlier disturbance.

11:28:27 Hours—Aboard the USS Memphis

Sonar operators in the sonar shack had no difficulty detecting or holding the acoustic picture that was being painted on their glowing screens. First was an undersea explosion. Then, a sub was blowing ballast for what seemed to be an emergency main ballast maneuver to surface the boat in the shortest possible time. Next came a jumble of sounds. Then, another explosion. The second was a blast of such magnitude the men on duty must have been thankful for the recordings that were being made, otherwise many might have believed they were exaggerating.

11:29:35 Hours—Aboard the Peter the Great

The sonar watch officer stared at the lines zigzagging up and down on the screen, stunned by their height and frequency. He'd never seen anything like this. To a trained eye, the tracings were as readable as a TV picture. He was viewing an explosion. And from the size of the blast, he knew everyone else in the area was receiving the same signals. Seismic waves from an incident this big were being recorded halfway around the world.

The precise location was easy to fix by using the reports from a number of ships and triangulation. Working together with the others, he quickly transferred the coordinates to a map, plotted a rough position, and marked it. The assessment of the several reporting sites was the same. It had been a small explosion followed by an enormous second blast.

NORSAR Observatory

A quick analysis of the data indicated an initial blast at 11:28:27, which registered 1.5 on the Richter scale. This was judged to be the equivalent of 220 pounds of explosives. A second, far more violent incident occurred at 11:30:42, resulting in a 3.5 Richter scale reading. Best estimates were that one to two tons of TNT detonated underwater would be needed to create an event of such magnitude.

For the experts gathered at the observatory, those facts presented a bleak picture. They were about to discover their instruments had recorded the death knell of one of the world's most deadly undersea weapons.

Later, after a detailed report was developed, Frode

Ringdair, a scientific adviser, was quoted as saying, "This was the single most powerful explosion we have ever registered in this area."

1131 Hours—Aboard the Kursk

Commander Lyachin's desperate effort to surface had momentarily appeared successful. The downward slant of the deck leveled, then slowly began to tilt in the other direction. They were coming up. The boat was sluggish but was answering the helm.

There was no time for elation. Action was their only salvation. Then, in one tick of a clock, action was not enough.

Reports on experiments by engineers at Dagdizel had indicated that the liquid-fueled torpedoes could withstand exposure to fire a little over two minutes. Continued heating beyond that point caused the fuel to boil, vaporize, and release large quantities of hydrogen gas. The resulting explosion would pack tremendous power.

Apparently, their engineering estimate was accurate. About 135 seconds after the first explosion, which started savage fires in Compartment 1, a second torpedo blew up. This blast initiated a chain reaction of explosions, recorded by surrounding vessels and NORSAR.

The force of this exploding arsenal was horrific. A gaping hole was blown in one side of the *Kursk*, lifting back a large flap of steel like a fish opening its mouth to strike. Through this fissure hot gas burst forth into the sea. Water adjacent to the hull turned to instant steam from the explosive heat. The resulting "bubble" shot to the surface, erupting in a geyser hundreds of feet high.

Cooling almost as soon as it boiled, seawater flooded into the submarine and was stopped by the emergency watertight sealing systems.

No one in the first five compartments was alive to respond to this devastation.

As before, when the torpedo tube contained the initial blast and directed the hellish energy, the interior of the pressurized hull now assumed the same role. An unstoppable shock wave, accompanied by a fireball of intense heat, flared through the submarine. Watertight doors sealing off the first five compartments could not hold against this insane pressure. As bulkheads were bowed, door seals failed and the explosive force rolled on.

Even more deadly, though, was the incandescent gas that shot through the ventilation system, sending gouts of fire into every compartment of the *Kursk*.

The third-generation nuclear reactors on board were a major advance over their predecessors. As electrical connections melted, the built-in safety features of the reactor modules automatically activated. Before heat could build in the pile, the control rods were shoved to their fully inserted positions, dampening the atomic activity. This action stopped the formation of steam, so the turbines slowed, then spun to a halt, stilling the huge twin props.

In spite of the blown ballast tanks, the submarine was nose heavy with inrushing sea. So the *Kursk* sank bowdown through the chilling water. The heavy vessel struck bottom with tons of force, scattering debris in a wide circle and sending up a thick curtain of primordial ooze. All was silent. In time, the sediment, carried by a small current, spread and settled. The deep now held the *Kursk* in a final embrace.

1133 Hours—Aboard the USNS Loyal

The sensitive undersea pickups deployed by the surveillance team relayed blast information to the many
recorders on board. And the crew found no problem iden-
tifying the source of the event. In the following minutes,
new sounds, easy for trained ears to decipher, told a
nightmarish story. As all propulsion died, the noise of
propeller cavitation or turbulence was replaced by the almost whalelike chorus of moans and shrill shrieks produced by metal flexing under massive stress.

The team of scientists and technicians hurriedly dupli-
cated the recordings of their findings. They would be relayed to the National Maritime Intelligence Center in
Suitland, Maryland, as quickly as possible. Dubs were
not as good as original tracks but would suffice to get an
investigation started.

An original recording of the event could also come
from either of the two U.S. submarines, the British sub
working the area, or the Norwegian *Marjata*. All would
have detailed records of the explosions and sinking. The
Memphis was scheduled to stop in Norway. From there,
tapes and disks would be flown back to the States.

Aboard the Kursk

Dmitry had been writing. He might not have wanted to think "last thoughts," but it would have been difficult not to do so.

Putting words on paper probably caused him to recall the foreboding he'd had about this cruise. He hadn't wanted to worry Olechka with his premonitions of disaster. It was difficult enough for her to remain behind while he sailed in harm's way.

They had decided he should leave the submarines. A position in science or engineering at one of the St. Petersburg Navy installations would be an ideal new assignment. It was not an easy decision. As a married man, he had responsibilities, as a submariner, obligations.

Before she had opened his emotional side, leaving the submarines would have been unthinkable, the loss in his life too great. Now she had filled that void.

On the day he departed St. Petersburg for this duty, he had left her a set of his identity tags, a crucifix, and a poem. One line vowed his love, declaring he could silently drown in her eyes.

By this point, Dmitry's trained and disciplined mind had accepted the truth. The odds on their making it were now very low.

That reality must have angered him. They weren't down that deep. And the explosions had to have been noted. So help should be on the way. Where were they?

Dmitry's life had been spared during the original blast of explosions and flames. And for what? The facts were there to face. If the Kursk had been less badly savaged, he and the rest might have had a chance. The damage was there, though, so it was only a matter of hours. And that understanding may have brought him peace.

By this point, Dmitry's head was aching, his mouth dry, and the contaminated air must have burned in his lungs. His friend, Rashid, had been writing as well. "We feel bad . . . we're weakened by the effects of carbon monoxide from the fire . . ." Dmitry would have concurred. The devastating flames that had flared through every portion of the submarine consumed precious oxygen at a horrendous rate. It had left an air poisoned with carbon monoxide.

The survivors could now feel the effects of increasing air pressure in their ears. That condition had been explained clearly during training. Building air pressure indicated seawater was pouring into the boat. As the water entered, under hundreds of pounds of pressure from the depths, great bubbles of air were forced upward until trapped against the steel hull. Then, slowly but inexorably, breathable gas was being squeezed tighter and tighter by the rising waters, raising the pressure.

Rashid had written, "Pressure is increasing in the compartment . . . if we head for the surface, we won't survive the compression. We won't last for more than a day.

Their living space was damp and they could see their breath as they exhaled stale air. The situation had worsened by the hour and now most of them knew they would not be able to remain alive long enough for the Deep Sea Rescue Vehicles to be brought to the scene. The only way out was through the double-hatch escape chute—which was a form of suicide.

Where were their rescuers? Why hadn't they come?

CHAPTER 5

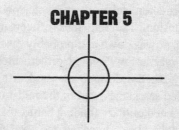

12 August 2000—Barents Sea

LEADERS OF THE NORTHERN FLEET AND RUSSIAN NAVY were confronted with a series of disconcerting facts.

First, there had been an enormous undersea explosion. Second, the blast had originated in a sector assigned to the *Kursk* for patrol. Third, at least one officer on board the *Peter the Great*, and probably a great many more, was aware that a missile had been fired and that it struck the sea, causing an unusually dramatic eruption of water. Fourth, only a large attack submarine carried sufficient weaponry to produce such a hellacious submerged blast. Fifth, Captain Lyachin had called for permission to release a faulty torpedo. That transmission, according to the media, was picked up by the USNS *Loyal*. So there can be little doubt the call was made and that ranking officers on board the *Peter the Great* knew this.

Finally, the *Peter the Great*, a sophisticated heavy nuclear missile cruiser, had first-class submarine-detection abilities. It was operating in a full combat mode with all of its electronic gear searching for the *Kursk*. So it is likely the *Kursk*, along with other submarines in the area, was being tracked. If so, the explosions would have knocked the *Kursk* "off the scope."

This information, taken as a whole, pointed to one strong conclusion. The flag rank officers immediately knew the *Kursk* was down and probably disabled.

Admiral Vyacheslav Popov, Northern Fleet commander, certainly faced a difficult reality. During his fleet's much heralded sea games, and in the midst of an important governmental military funding battle, the pride of the Russian Navy had been damaged and possibly even lost. This situation confronted the admiral with several interrelated hard alternatives.

As an old submariner, he would have had instant concern for those on board the *Kursk*. And he would have known that survivors were trained to hold out as long as possible for help to arrive. In the U.S. Navy, sailors are aware they might have to sustain themselves for up to a week. Russian submariners must have about the same time horizon. While a week may seem an inordinate period, especially because many preparations are already in place and set for immediate use, massing for a deep-water rescue mission is an extremely complex operation. Every precaution must be taken to keep from endangering the lives of the rescuers as well as the trapped personnel.

So the admiral's first decision concerned the unleashing of a full-fledged search-and-rescue mission. While any delay might result in the unnecessary loss of lives, ordering immediate action also presented problems.

Every rescue effort is an expensive undertaking. To

initiate such an action without being certain about conditions on board the *Kursk* could be wasteful. Standard operating procedures also supported a delay. The *Kursk* had a strict reporting schedule. If the submarine did not contact Fleet HQ at the specified time, still some hours away, then a problem had to be assumed. There also might be the possibility of receiving an SOS from the sub. She was equipped with an automatic emergency deployment buoy with a built-in identifier. A signal for help would immediately trigger a rescue mission.

The Navy could wait, a short while, for the *Kursk* to call at her scheduled reporting time or send an SOS. The submarine might be only slightly damaged. Or, a weak possibility, she might simply be maintaining radio silence.

Moreover, security presented an obstacle to dispatching an immediate rescue effort. As soon as the first Russian ship began working a search pattern, U.S. eyes and NATO ears would be alerted. Both the Russian press and foreign observers would suspect the Northern Fleet had an emergency.

Time was also needed for another purpose. Flag rank officers are obligated to keep political realities in mind before acting. Key military and governmental figures had to be notified and brought into the situation. This was Russia, and it was imperative officials agree on a course of action. If the *Kursk* was down, the need to blame someone would be intense. If lives were lost as well, finding fault would become a passion. A disaster of this magnitude could shake the military and political foundations of the nation.

In his role as one of the highest ranking officers in the

Russian Navy, Admiral Popov was dealing with many serious considerations. At the same time, he had to remember that any delay in a rescue effort would result in a massive morale problem with submariners throughout his command. Other factors undoubtedly also influenced the final decision. In spite of all that was known and suspected, no rescue effort was initiated at that point in the drama.

Admiral Popov's departure from the *Peter the Great* shortly after the explosion was in all probability to reach a secure communications link with the commander in chief of the Russian Navy, Admiral Vladimir Kuroyedov. Popov's report was one that needed to be made without any chance of eavesdroppers. And there were plenty of potential listeners, ranging from NATO, the U.S., the news media, and intelligence units of other Russian military services.

Until an official position could be established, it was imperative that no one outside a select few have even an inkling anything was wrong. The potential for damaging the Navy, personal careers, and worldwide Russian prestige was horrendous.

Even senior naval officers were not immune from the need to avoid admission of error. The slightest comment that could be taken as accepting the smallest responsibility for an accident could turn the whole disaster into that person's fault.

And in today's Russia, there is a new wild card. Since the fall of the Soviet Union, the news media, once so tightly caged, is now loose in the streets. A story with the dramatic potential of a Navy miscue and an undersea rescue would cause the newshounds to salivate. One leak of a story this spectacular, and there would be no stopping them.

All this made one point clear. Eventually, someone, something, or some organization was going to be held accountable for this tragedy. To avoid being blamed, a great many officials were going to have to avoid the truth through the use of half-truths or outright lies.

August 12—1330 Hours—On Board the Peter the Great

Activities relating to the sea maneuvers continued. To halt the exercise would have focused instant attention on the situation—and produced unanswerable questions.

The *Peter the Great* and her protective convoy proceeded to operate as a unit, turning this way and that to maintain their evasionary tactics. As the day progressed, with no practice torpedoes fired at them from the *Kursk*, the ship's crew had to wonder why they were not attacked. Among those who knew or suspected the reason, concern for the lost sub grew.

The *Kursk*'s schedule called for her to make a report to Northern Fleet HQ not later than 1800 hours. Until then, she was supposed to have remained in combat hunt-and-kill training conditions.

Time passed slowly. As hour after hour slogged by, the air of anticipation and worry had intensified. While only a few knew or had reason to suspect the worst, they must have wordlessly communicated their concerns. Even among those who possessed all the facts, there was some hope. Maybe the *Kursk* was stuck on the bottom with propulsion troubles. Perhaps she was playing a trick on them by remaining silent. Or possibly she'd been crippled and had limped secretly back to home port. That would make sense. The Navy would maintain radio silence to keep news of damage to the submarine quiet. No sense revealing problems to the Americans or NATO.

Rumors are a staple form of entertainment in every nation's military. And, as rumors do, they began to multiply. Vague misgivings grew into plausible theories and even the thinnest bit of information was transformed to fit one or another scenario.

As the 1800-hour deadline for the *Kursk* to report approached, plans were being laid in high places.

Under the rule of the Union of Soviet Socialist Republics, handling this situation would have been a relatively simple issue. In many previous submarine disasters the loss was simply not mentioned outside a need-to-know group. Under the old regime, no information was released to the news media. Any stories that leaked out were flatly denied. Families were told nothing—or, at best, given notice that a loved one had been lost in action. And that report, in many instances, did not come until years after the event. There were no investigations, no public hearings, nothing. Justification for this attitude stemmed from the concept that every citizen was in essence a ward of the state. Therefore every citizen owed allegiance and even life to the state.

In Russia today, actions are directed by a somewhat different, more humane viewpoint. Freedom and democratic rule by law were concepts that had taken root. Those principles also provided the basis for personal independence and opportunity.

Old ways and attitudes are often difficult to forget, however, especially when they are more expedient, convenient, or serve a desired end. It appears that to some degree, a clash between the old and the new caused many of the difficulties related to the *Kursk* disaster.

For example, the Northern Fleet had to obey regulations. They might bend procedures a bit and cut a corner or two, but Navy regs had to be followed. There were severe consequences for deviating too much from the book. And the book demanded action in a set manner within a specified period of time. As a result, officials had to make big decisions within an initial time window that was very tight.

Second, naval command had to launch a concerted effort to deal with the media. What was to be released, and when, was crucial to keeping the situation from escalating into a circus. Coordination of news services was vital.

Then there was always the matter of fault finding. If the tragedy could be blamed on some foreign intervention, then the leaders involved would be safe. This ploy, perfected by the military and government of the Soviet Union, traded on creating a paranoia based on a threat of aggression from the West. It had worked famously in the past. There was no reason to abandon its use now.

Beyond that, and of potentially equal importance, came dealing with the families, maintaining Russian prestige, keeping a high level of morale in the Navy, not allowing the incident to become politically destabilizing, as well as a host of other vital issues.

Without doubt, the Navy high command was faced with an enormous responsibility. Hard choices had to be made—and be made quickly.

12 August 2000—1700 Hours—Northern Fleet HQ

The *Kursk*'s reporting deadline was 1800 hours and based on what was already known, it was senseless to wait until that time. More than five hours, used for hurried discussions and preliminary planning by the high command, had elapsed since the second blast.

To begin the operation, naval officials went to the rule book. At 1700 hours, the Northern Fleet Rescue Service chief on duty was notified that there might be a problem on board the *Kursk*. With this done, Northern Fleet HQ used a secure communications channel, and 30 minutes later, at 1730, sent an order to the *Kursk*: "Report your coordinates and operations."

The Navy procedure manual allows six hours for a response. Anxious officers and men, divided into parties for monitoring space communications, automatic communications, radio intelligence, telegraphy, and regular radio bands, dealt with every form of long-distance communications technique available.

No response was received.

In accordance with what Colonel-General Valeriy Manilov, first deputy chief of the Russian General Staff, was quoted as calling the "requirements of normative documents," the *Kursk* was declared to be in distress. A Northern Fleet emergency alarm was sounded. The time was 2330 hours. The date, Saturday, August 12, 2000, almost exactly 12 hours after the explosions.

This moment marked the commencement of one of the largest search-and-rescue investigatory salvage operations in the history of the Russian Navy.

At that point, no one knew actual conditions aboard the *Kursk*. Several high-ranking officers had strong suspicions, and rumors were rampant. Even though efforts had been made to prevent news of the accident from reaching the media, word of trouble travels fast in the military.

In Vidyaevo, the Navy village where so many of the submariners lived, families appeared to have known there was something wrong by 1700 hours on Saturday. More, a story passed from one to another was that the *Kursk* had been hit by a Russian missile during the exercises. The sub's fate was cloudy. Some said there had been great damage; others, more optimistic, believed the boat was still operational.

In an attempt to contain such gossip, and to leave communications links open, telephone service to the various residential enclaves was shut down. Only official calls were allowed in or, more important, out. Disruption of service effectively isolated these communities from the rest of the nation.

On a more heroic level, the men of the Northern Fleet Rescue Service went into action. Most of these sailors knew nothing of the loftier concerns being debated in high places. They assumed the *Kursk* was down. It was their job to save the lives of as many of the crew as possible.

A two-pronged operation was launched. One effort focused on finding the stricken vessel. The second was rapid deployment of ships and equipment needed to help those on board. Fortunately, the operating area assigned to the *Kursk* was known. There was no reason to assume the submarine had left its war games zone. So all activities for locating the vessel would be concentrated in that limited geographic area. This knowledge also allowed the

Rescue Service to transport its resources closer to where they would be needed.

A joint air-sea search was quickly instituted. A Russian officer, Lieutenant Colonel Dergunov, commanded one of the four-engined Ilyushin-38 aircraft. With a useful range of 4,500 miles, this workhorse plane was sufficiently fast and ideal for sea searches. Flying in formation with a fellow officer, Lieutenant Colonel Dovzhenko, commander of a second Il-38, this team began an aerial examination of the sector in question.

Aided by evening daylight, a visual inspection of the sea proved possible. This, coupled with use of onboard electronic gear, gave the two Il-38s a significant advantage.

Air reconnaissance may be both tedious and stressful. The passing of hours in a droning aircraft can be difficult enough. Fatigue comes from an endless scanning of water through binoculars, with hopes rising and falling at each unusual glint of light on the waves. Equally tiring is the ceaseless working up and down through various radio bands while static snaps and crackles in the earphones. Both these pursuits must be diligently performed or there is no use bothering to precision fly the checkerboard search coordinates and cover the selected site.

On board Lieutenant Colonel Dergunov's Ilyushin, which carries a normal crew of ten, men sat at their observation stations. As hours passed, the watchers and listeners had to stay alert. Any brief attention lapse might mean missing the lone clue that would unravel the mystery.

Then, suddenly, the searchers were successful. A large oil spill marred the sea. Map coordinates were relayed to

Northern Fleet HQ. According to unconfirmed reports, the pair of airborne spotters also saw a "foreign" submarine lurking underwater at five knots. And they supposedly sighted white and green emergency buoys. White and green are not the colors of Russian signaling devices, so these were determined to be from a sub of another nation.

The story of spotting a foreign sub and the emergency buoys marked the opening of a campaign to transfer any blame for the *Kursk* disaster from the Northern Fleet to another country. It's interesting that the buoys were later believed to be cabbage heads, but finally identified as a floating sack of potatoes. As for the mysterious submarine, it could have been one of the three U.S. or British boats monitoring the exercises. It might also have been misinformation designed to support shifting responsibility for the disaster.

Of greater political importance, however, was the confirmed sighting of two foreign P-3C Orion surveillance aircraft at or near the disaster site. Since NORSAR, the seismological observatory, had recorded the explosions, they had a precise fix on the location. Even nonscientific curiosity would have mandated a visual inspection of the area. Conveniently, there had been daily flights to observe Russian sea maneuvers. Since the planes were in the air already, making a quick check was simple.

The Orions flying over that particular spot in the ocean must have been troubling to those attempting to keep a lid on this situation. The presence of the two planes could be viewed as an indication that another government suspected there had been some kind of disaster associated with the sea exercises.

While the incident was highly confidential, the circle of people who knew of the *Kursk* sinking expanded beyond the military to include top government officials. That, in turn, spread the news, as seen through an action of the Russian Ministry of Foreign Affairs. Conscious of relations with Norway, a close neighbor on the Barents Sea, a Foreign Affairs minister contacted the appropriate Norwegian authorities and alerted them to a possible accident with a nuclear submarine.

12 August 2000—2350 Hours—On Board the Peter the Great

The effective underwater detection capabilities of the *Peter the Great* were brought into the hunt shortly after the rescue alarm was sounded in the fleet. With all available systems operating, the cruiser began a sea search to complement the air survey. Because of her speed and excellent equipment, the ship was able to quickly cover a large segment of the patrol area assigned to the *Kursk*. Likewise, the pair of undersea explosions that had been recorded by the sonar group gave a good indication of where to look.

A quick pinpoint location of the lost submarine was vital. Help was on the way from Fleet HQ in Severomorsk. Guiding the rescue fleet to the right spot could save hours and possibly lives. The flagship redoubled its radio watches and intensified efforts to contact the *K-141*.

12 August 2000—2100 Hours—Northern Fleet Rescue Service

Alexander Teslenko was head of the Rescue Service of the Northern Fleet. And at his disposal were a tugboat and two rescue vessels. One, the *Mikhail Rudnitsky*, had a sister ship undergoing repairs. Constructed in the Vyborg Shipyard in 1980, the *Rudnitsky* was modified from a lumber carrier. She was intended to serve as "mother ship" to a pair of Deep Submergence Rescue Vehicles (DSRVs).

Two DSRV designs were immediately available. The Briz-class minisubs were constructed between 1986 and 1989. Operated by a crew of four, this rescue vehicle attaches to the escape hatch of a sunken submarine and can carry as many as 20 passengers to safety. The smaller, later style Bester model uses the same system. Its crew of three is able to save 16 to 18 people at a time. The *Rudnitsky* was also equipped with a diving bell, underwater TV, lifting cranes, and other specialized gear. At full speed, she made 15.8 knots.

A DSRV is not a sleek, undersea boat. It looks like a huge industrial-grade boiler with a hatch projecting upward from the top. A large propeller at the rear is protected by a cowling. Snub-nosed, it is fitted with streamlined pods attached to the sides of the round vessel to handle air, ballast water, and other necessities. Ungainly on the surface, it is highly controllable when submerged. In addition to bright lights, they are equipped with sonar, electronic listening-detection devices, and other search-rescue gear.

The Northern Fleet also had one rescue submarine with the NATO designation of India. This boat was specifically designed for undersea rescue work and is capable of carrying two DSRVs. In a St. Petersburg yard for repairs, it could not be utilized on this mission.

Without waiting for the *Kursk*'s 2300-hour reporting deadline, Teslenko began immediate preparations. The captain of the *Rudnitsky*, docked at Severomorsk, the main Northern Fleet base, received orders to stand by. He was to be ready for departure on 60-minute notice. The captain immediately loaded and checked the pair of Briz-type DSRVs. By 2220 hours he was set to leave.

The *Altay*, a second vessel, was designed to support divers, tow grounded ships to deeper water, rescue people in the sea, and work above sunken vessels. She was ordered into one-hour readiness as well.

The tug, which had been near Kildin Island, had been dispatched to the *Kursk*'s patrol zone much earlier, at 1831. It would take four hours to make the trip.

When the deadline for the *Kursk* to report had passed, Teslenko wasted no time. He hurried aboard the *Rudnitsky*. Moments later, they cast off all lines and, at full speed, started their dash for the *Kursk*'s patrol area.

13 August 2000—0430 Hours—Aboard the Peter the Great

Deep inside the *Peter the Great*, in a red-lighted room far from the tranquility of sea and sky, specialists and technicians were hard at work. The sonar and electronic scanning had continued for several hours. Using coordinates provided by the search aircraft and their previous plot estimates from the explosions, the flagship had been making its own checkerboard pattern.

Shortly before 0436 hours on Sunday, August 13, a sonar operator caught an anomaly on his screen. Tense moments followed as others joined in and they enriched their findings by changing angles and moving closer. One after another, features began to match the profile of *K-141*. Moments later, there was agreement. They had located the *Kursk* on the sea floor. But was that all they found?

According to a document from the Russian Navy Museum, a submarine operated for the Main Intelligence Department appeared at the site. This boat remained in the area for several hours. It inspected the bow of the damaged *Kursk* during the night of August 12 and morning of August 13. High Russian officials later denied that this investigation took place. Sketchy naval records indicate it did. And if it did, which seems probable, the high command had credible information about the extent of damage their submarine had suffered.

In any case, based on some form of positive identification and, again according to a Russian Navy Museum document, Minister of Defense Igor Sergeyev was notified. At 0700 hours on August 13, Sergeyev contacted President Vladimir V. Putin and explained the *Kursk* emergency. Putin was vacationing in the southern resort town of Sochi on the Black Sea. During this talk, the Defense minister "did not recommend him to arrive on a crash scene." This is an important point. In the turbulent political fallout to follow, Putin would be severely criticized for not ending his holiday and personally going to the rescue site.

In truth, Putin's presence, while lending a morale element to the effort, would have had little practical value. A major salvage and rescue mission had begun. Admiral

Popov was assuming direct command from his *Peter the Great* flagship. And all available resources were on the way.

Another issue also emerged. The Russian president cutting short his vacation for a sudden trip to the Barents Sea would have whetted the interest of the news media. No press announcement regarding the *Kursk* had been made. At this point the Navy, as it later did, could cite the uncertainty of the situation as a defense for not releasing information. The question, however, is just how much uncertainty remained? Between sonar and other electronic evaluations performed by the *Peter the Great*, and quite possibly observations made by an intelligence department submarine, a great deal must have been known about the *Kursk*'s condition.

On a separate note, yet related to this question of knowledge, Admiral Vladimir Kuroyedov, commander in chief of the entire Russian Navy, reportedly tendered his resignation on the night of August 12. Clearly, the top officer in the Navy is not expected to resign every time a ship is lost. Tragedy or not, military vessels sail in harm's way. They are heavily armed and, in spite of all possible care, accidents happen. Why then, would Admiral Kuroyedov make such an offer? Was it because he, and others in high command, knew the cause and extent of damage sustained by the *Kursk*? Did they have a sound estimate of the fate of the crew? That information, if they possessed it, may well have been reason enough to resign.

As an opposing concept, resignations are offered in Russia for many reasons. One of the best is to determine support levels. Refusing an offer to resign can indicate

solidarity or a willingness to work with the person re-
signing. If the Navy had settled on a strategy of blaming
foreigners for the loss of their submarine, refusal might
well indicate tacit agreement with that plan.

Even in the face of evidence to the contrary, select members of the Russian Navy upper echelon appear to have
taken a stand. Their position was that the *Kursk* was sunk
due to a collision with a foreign vessel. It was first suggested that one of the two U.S. submarines had been involved. That was later changed to focus on the *Splendid*,
from Great Britain. In either case, a foreign sub was at fault.

13 August 2000—0839 Hours—On Board the Rudnitsky

Driven by a sense of urgency, Alexander Teslenko and
his group made good time on their voyage from Severomorsk. Once inside the perimeter of the *Kursk* patrol
area, they began an all-wavelength search for radio signals from the lost submarine. By noon they had temporarily anchored to continue this effort.

In keeping with regulations, they realized there was a
possibility that surviving crewmen might not know the
many reporting codes and radio frequencies. So they
started using open-microphone verbal messages in their
quest. There was still no response.

At the same time, they were prepping *AS-34*, one of
the DSRV submersibles. Further contact with the *Peter
the Great* gave them a solid fix on the location of the discovered anomaly. So they hurried to that position, ready
to place *AS-34* into the cold, dark water.

Aboard the Kursk

Sitting, staring straight ahead, Dmitry must have realized the constant striving for perfection and total devotion to duty he'd allowed to dominate his life were, in these final hours, of no avail. His last comfort had come from the emotions he'd so avoided.

Loving Olechka had changed him. It was not magic, yet the shift had come overnight. It was as if he'd gone to sleep the ideal officer who placed perfect performance and duty ahead of all else. Then he awakened with the realization there was another, equally if not more important set of values. He'd been touched by a new understanding of what was truly vital in life. His love for Olechka had revealed a fresh horizon. His images of her were soft and fine and beautiful.

One by one, the emergency lights faded from sharp incandescence to reddish brown and went out. Dmitry, shivering in blackness from the clammy, bone-chilling cold, wrote again. "It is dark to write here, but I will try to do it blindly. It looks that there are no chances—10 to 20 percent. We will hope that somebody will read this.”

He must have been momentarily distracted by the constant gurgle of relentless water seeping into the boat. It would have been difficult to ignore the sound and write another line. The air was almost totally contaminated and could not sustain them much longer.

Dmitry, supported by memories that evoked long-denied feelings in his heart, had somehow managed to control his pencil. *“Olechka, I love you . . . here are the lists of the personnel of the departments who are located in the ninth section and will be trying to get out. Hello to everybody. Don’t despair.”*

Dmitry would have been tempted to add his usual closing line, “Embrace and kisses.” Instead, he turned the paper over and by feel located a place to write one last time.

“Olechka, I love you. Don’t be too upset. Say hello to GV. Say hello to my family, too. Mitya.” She would be pleased he’d remembered her mom, GV.

Dmitry could be glad now for the poem he’d written and included in the package he’d left with his beautiful wife. It contained a promise. In his mind, recall of the final words in the last stanza had to have been clear. *“And when the time comes to die, though I chase such thoughts away, I want time to whisper one thing: ‘My darling, I love you.’ ”*

In the lonely darkness that was now so full of the love that came from his heart, he probably spoke aloud, in a quiet voice. “My darling, I love you.” His pledge to Olechka had been fulfilled.

CHAPTER 6

13 August 2000—Early Morning
Barents Sea

FLYING HIGH ABOVE THE BARENTS SEA, THE NORWEGIAN crew aboard the Lockheed Orion P-3C/N surveillance aircraft began their regular morning sortie. A direct descendant of the old and short-lived Electra passenger airliner, the Orion is the workhorse of maritime patrols and one of the world's best antisubmarine-warfare weapons platforms. The term "weapons platform" is used by the military to describe the plane, boat, tank, or other device used to carry various weaponry and deliver that armament to the place where it may be utilized against an enemy. Four powerful turboprop engines allow the Orion to fly search patterns covering thousands of miles without refueling. It can carry up to eight tons of payload composed of electronics gear, sensors, torpedoes, depth charges, and rockets.

On this flight, the plane was not armed for combat.

The crew was there, as they had been every day since the Russian sea games began, to observe. The heart of their observation system was called the Tactical Coordinator or TACCO station. Occupying a space on the port side of the aircraft just behind the flight deck, the TACCO operator had all the information being collected by the plane's many sensors displayed on a single large screen.

The Russian Fleet's disposition was expected to be similar to yesterday's. It wasn't. The ships below appeared to have abandoned their war games.

A radio link to Norway's *Marjata* electronics intelligence ship, which by some accounts had been leased to the CIA, helped clarify the movement patterns. Many of the vessels seemed to be engaged in a search exercise.

13 August 2000—1615 Hours—On Board the Rudnitsky

The immensely powerful DSRV submersible bore the service number *AS-34*. She was classified as a Briz, which designated her size and capabilities. A little over 30 feet in length and 12 feet wide, she packed a lot of technology into a small space. Her battery-powered motors could drive her slightly more than 3 knots. At a lower speed of 2.3 knots, maximum range was 21 miles. She was also able to lift and carry other vessels weighing up to 60 tons.

The *AS-34* could dive to a maximum depth of just over 3,000 feet and remain submerged between two and three hours. Those capabilities were more than enough for this mission.

Being lowered into the water from the deck of the *Rudnitsky* was a trying experience. As noted previously, the mother ship had originally been designed as a lumber carrier. Extensive modifications had been made to allow it to perform its present mission. And while the conversion was adequate, the seamen had to exercise great caution to prevent damage to the DSRVs.

Once safely floating in the sea, the *AS-34* crew hurried to submerge. The shape of their craft made it susceptible to wave motion while surfaced. Pitching and rolling were acute. Working quickly, they established a radio link with the *Rudnitsky*, performed the balance of their prediving checks, and were ready.

Motors whirring, the minisub gently slid beneath the waves. As the boat descended, light from the sky above began to fade from clear to a gentle violet to deep blue. At a depth of 200 feet, there was total darkness. Even with the running lamps and main spotlight, vision was limited because of stirred silt. The crew knew that nearer the bottom it would be even worse.

Several electric heaters kept the inside of the rescue sub reasonably warm. As she went deeper, it would grow colder.

In reporting conditions to the surface, comments were made about the low visibility. All were thankful they had an electronics trick that could lead them to the *Kursk*. Otherwise, they might spend days hunting blind.

Flying the small submersible required constant attention because of variable undersea currents. The ride, though, was smooth, and changes in direction or depth were as easy to make as in a light plane.

The pilot was searching for a place with negligible current at a depth of about 200 feet. When he found it, he aligned the boat by compass so that it was pointing in the same direction as the *Rudnitsky*, far above them on the surface.

Easing back slowly on the throttle and adjusting their buoyancy brought the DSRV to a complete stop. To execute the plan, the minisub would lie quiet. Experts on board the *Rudnitsky* would then send out a strong sonic probe or ping and a radio signal. There was an automatic acoustic station on board the *Kursk*. If the probe hit it right, there would be a response ping from the sub. The crew would then record and home on that signal.

With the motors stilled, it was quiet inside *AS-34*—so quiet in the deep it was possible for the men to hear their own heartbeats. Then the *Rudnitsky*'s probe, ringing like the metallic ting of a spoon hitting a crystal goblet, was loud in the minisub. At 1620 hours, there was a solid response.

Working frantically to intercept the contacts being traded between the *Kursk* and *Rudnitsky*, *AS-34* powered cautiously forward, then back, then to one side. All the while, the electronics specialist on board tried to align his equipment with the generated signals. It took over an hour. At 1748, they had their lock. It was tight enough to give them a proper fix.

Easing ahead through the blackness was like driving a car on a strange road at night in a dense fog. Their lights were absorbed by the silted water. At times, visibility was less than a yard.

Speed was now measured in feet instead of miles per hour. Then the sonar indicated a monstrous shape dead ahead.

Disaster struck at about 1830 hours. With a horrendous steel-slamming clang, the minisub gave a jolting lurch. They had hit the *Kursk*. Their impact point was, as best they could tell, on one of the sub's large steering wings.

Fear of serious damage caused a hasty safety assessment. Fortunately, only a few leaks were found. Their hull remained intact.

In spite of calling the situation an emergency, they made another pass. This time they lucked into a clearer view. With this visual confirmation, they contacted their mother ship. A satellite fix was taken on their location and the rescue fleet had the *Kursk*'s precise coordinates. After recording the depth, water temperature, and the angle between the sub and the sea floor, they were satisfied they'd done all they could on this first trip and surfaced.

After a few minutes of jockeying for position, the *AS-34* submersible was hooked onto a crane and lifted from the water back to the *Rudnitsky*'s decks.

According to a statement attributed to Alexander Teslenko, the exact seabed location of the *Kursk* was established in 6 hours and 27 minutes after the search party had been dispatched—a commendable feat.

While the crew quickly made their reports, a repair team swung into action. *AS-34* would be needed again in this rescue mission. As work proceeded, two other operations were given top priority.

The *Rudnitsky* once again changed locations. The ship now assumed a position over the site of the wreck. The second DSRV, registered as *AS-32*, was readied for use.

Other ships had been arriving, including the rescue team's tugboat and the *Altay*, which managed twice to deploy a diving bell. Shaped like an early space capsule, a bell acts as a kind of undersea elevator. Divers breathing normal air can remain at depths of more than 300 feet only a few minutes due to the pressure on their bodies. They ride in the bell, which is kept at the standard one atmosphere and lowered quickly. Once on the bottom, they venture out for the allotted maximum safe period. Then they reenter the bell and are lifted back to the surface.

Since the bell on the *Altay* was used, the Russians clearly had divers on or near the *Kursk*. Contrary to published reports insisting the high command of the Northern Fleet did not yet know the actual condition of the *Kursk*, the presence of divers, along with other evidence, indicates the opposite. Divers were sent to survey the damage and, by hammering on the hull, attempt to determine if there were any survivors.

Sea and weather conditions remained good and the early success boosted morale—as did a rumor. Some were saying there had been sounds from the *Kursk*. The knocking was like someone hammering in Morse code on the inside hull. The tapping was weak and reportedly read "SOS. Water." Recordings were made for better analysis. No one was sure if these sounds were actually signals. The possibility brought hope.

Aboard the Peter the Great

A very thoughtful Admiral Popov, who had assumed overall command of the rescue operation, had returned to his flagship, the *Peter the Great*. The decision had been made to focus on recovery of personnel aboard the lost submarine. It is possible and even probable that certain individuals already knew any rescue activity was a lost cause. Even if they did, sending aid was the best option. When word of the disaster reached the news media, it would be imperative to have more than the appearance of an effort to save lives.

Press notification merited top attention. The first question that would be asked by the news media was obvious. What had happened? The initial answer to that query was established. The *Kursk* was lost because of a collision with a foreign vessel—probably a submarine. When the time came to inform the press, the collision response had to be introduced by high-ranking individuals. This would serve to increase the veracity of that position. No less a personage than Deputy Prime Minister Ilya Klebanov, who was soon to be named chief of the government commission appointed to investigate the disaster, was one of the earliest, if not the first, proponents of the collision theory in the media.

The "foreign sub" story had to be uppermost in everyone's mind during this operation, because any hard evidence that could support the collision theory would make that position more believable. So every opportunity to search for "proof" had to be taken.

A well-conceived political damage-control program must also offer other reasonable explanations for the disaster. These help create a diversity of public opinion, thus confusing the issue. Alternate causes also provide failsafe positions in case the main theory does not catch on or cannot be proven. There was only one prime requirement for all the officially recognized possibilities. None could cast blame on the Navy or Russian government.

For certain, the press was going to demand answers. And if enough facts were not forthcoming, reporters would dig until some were found—or worse, use flights of fancy to explain the cause of the catastrophe.

Another burning problem came from the ever-present danger of leakage from a damaged nuclear reactor. While the disaster was bad enough, the situation would grow far worse if there was nuclear contamination. Release of radiation was of immediate importance because the Barents Sea was one of the world's most productive fishing areas.

The Navy would be in a much stronger position if positive assurances of proper reactor shutdown could be given as part of the initial release. This produced an urgent need to collect samples of seawater and metal from the *Kursk*'s hull. These specimens could then be analyzed to determine if any danger existed. So sample gathering was an important part of the rescue effort.

In the early evening hours of Sunday, August 13, as activity at the *Kursk* site was building, Admiral Popov appeared on Russian national TV. From the deck of the *Peter the Great*, he declared that the Northern Fleet's sea war games had been a resounding success. No mention was made of the *Kursk*.

Popov's televised comments of that night would be remembered later and cause a major backlash. The official explanation for this seemingly devious act was that Popov's remarks had been recorded earlier, before the *Kursk* disaster, and played on the Sunday show. That story is most likely true. No one, however, canceled the use of this prerecorded tape, which plainly shows a tendency to manipulate the news. And inadvertently or on purpose, that is precisely what was to happen.

2240 Hours—On Board the Rudnitsky

AS-32, the second DSRV, was successfully deployed over the side. Her mission was to get close-up television pictures of the wreck and especially the escape hatch to the ninth compartment.

During the next two and a half hours, the crew, hampered by poor visibility, made several descents. Proceeding cautiously, to minimize damage to their boat if they collided with the lost sub, they searched quadrant after quadrant. In spite of known precise coordinates, *AS-32*, for some unexplained reason, failed to make visual contact with its target.

Pressure to hurry the rescue effort was growing by the hour. So the now-repaired *AS-34* submersible was rushed back into action.

The crew once again managed to locate the downed submarine, but was forced to resurface because of drained batteries. This setback brought about a costly, expedient decision.

In normal conditions, a complete recharge of DSRV onboard batteries takes some 13 to 14 hours. This period can be shortened, but doing so seriously depletes the useful life of the battery packs. Since these are expensive to replace, deciding to do a quick hotshot recharge demonstrates the urgency everyone was feeling.

Back in the water less than 60 minutes later, the crew went directly to the sunken vessel. *AS-34* cautiously maneuvered to the stern escape hatch and made its first attempt to dock. Their goal was to mate with the hatch, open it from inside the DSRV, and thereby establish a dry escape route for trapped personnel.

The crew worked without break for almost three

hours, using up much of their breathable air. They were unable to mount a rescue. A combination of poor visibility, undersea currents, the angle at which the *Kursk* rested on the bottom, and damage to the escape hatch docking flange, were all said to have played a role in the failure.

Since the *Kursk* was not lying horizontally, it was decided a later model DSRV, one of the two Bester (*AS-36*) units, would be better suited for the docking job. That model was designed to mate with a surface at an angle up to 45 degrees and could remain submerged a full four hours. An emergency call was put through ordering the deep submersible to the rescue site.

14 August 2000—1015 Hours

A large number of people were becoming involved in the rescue activity—which made keeping the loss a secret from the media progressively more difficult. The telephone censorship placed on Vidyaevo and some of the other villages where Northern Fleet personnel lived was also attracting media curiosity. Fearful of a leak, officials believed the best policy was to control information by making a preliminary press release. It was decided that the initial announcement did not have to reveal the actual nature of the situation. That could wait until the question of radiation leakage was resolved—and, it was hoped, after some evidence was found to back up the collision story.

Two days after the disaster, on Monday, August 14, at 1045 hours, the Navy Press Center issued the first public statement: ". . . there were malfunctions on the submarine, therefore she was compelled to lay on a seabed in region of Northern Fleet exercises in Barents Sea."

While that account was not, on a word for word basis, a direct lie, it certainly did not reveal the seriousness of the accident. The first release also noted that the incident had occurred on Sunday, August 13, rather than Saturday, August 12.

Further information, this time a bit less truthful, indicated communications with the submarine were said to be working.

Shortly after noon, Vice Admiral Einar Skorgen, Commander North Norway (COMNON), used the red telephone in his office at COMNON headquarters located at Reitan. The facility was built deep inside a nuclear bombproof complex excavated from an Arctic mountain near the Norwegian town of Bodoe. Skorgen activated the direct line to Admiral Popov. This new straight-through link had been established in April 1999 to further relations between the neighboring nations. It had never before been used. Acting under orders from the Norwegian Ministry of Defense, Admiral Skorgen, through an interpreter, requested details on the *Kursk* situation. He also offered direct assistance as well as a willingness to coordinate aid from NATO.

The Russian response was gracious and clear. Thanks, but no thanks. The matter was under control. No help was required.

At this point, that answer most probably summed up an honest attitude. The Northern Fleet had ample resources on-site and more assistance on the way. If the Navy high command knew the actual condition of the

Kursk, such experienced men of flag and even lower rank would be able to perform their own damage assessment. Loss of a large percentage of the crew would be a foregone conclusion. The need for even more help would be hard to justify.

Besides, bringing in the Norwegians, or any foreigners at this junction, would have served as the detonator for a news media explosion. Worse, it would be an admission of Russian inability to care for her own men. And almost as bad, asking for help was like passing out an open invitation for any interested party to come and examine the most advanced submarine in their Navy.

1400 Hours—Rescue Site

NTV, the Russian independent television network, broke into its regular programming with a special bulletin. The *Kursk* was down. The submarine's bow was damaged and flooded. All power generation on board the boat had been cut.

Armed with the Navy Press Office release, reporters had gone to work. At least one, and most likely more people with knowledge of the disaster, talked. Since few knew the extent of damage, there was a good probability that the someone who spoke was a ranking officer.

Two hours after the NTV report, the Navy denied any flooding and again placed the time of the incident on Sunday.

Apparently pressure from the news media developed rapidly. Two hours after the second Navy statement, Admiral Vladimir Kuroyedov, chief of the Russian Navy, admitted the *Kursk* was seriously damaged.

At the site, divers obtained water samples to check for radiation. Thus far, no contamination was detected. That was the only bright spot, because the deep-sea TV camera modules, which carry their own light sources, provided pictures that indicated vastly more damage to the submarine's front sections than had been anticipated. The Navy made no mention of this distressing fact.

By this time, and because of other Navy press confusion, obfuscation, and falsehoods, their Public Information Office credibility had been damaged. As the evening progressed, the foreign-sub ramming theory was offered as actual fact. There was also talk of an explosion on board. Denials and counterdenials abounded. Offers of help from foreign governments poured in.

Britain agreed to loan its LR-5 DSRV. This rescue vehicle had been modified when it was used to assist a Polish sub. Its escape hatch matched the Polish model, which was much like the Russian design.

The U.S., NATO, and Norway were all quick to volunteer aid. These offers produced another quandary for the Russian group orchestrating how the disaster could best be handled in terms of protecting careers, Navy image, and honor.

To accept help could well be construed as an admission that the Navy was incapable of doing the job. It would also sting national pride.

To refuse assistance might lay officials open to later charges of callous disregard for human life—especially if it was discovered that crewmen on the downed boat lived for days and the rescue work proceeded too slowly to save them.

To further complicate a messy situation, there was the

question of equipment compatibility. With the exception of the modified British submersible, fittings of other nations would be incompatible with Russian gear. Therefore time had to be spent determining what outside aid might be useful and how best to employ those resources. Starting such discussions would immediately demonstrate a willingness to accept help, even though that assistance might not, after serious consideration, be beneficial.

The place to review possible help was NATO. Most of the nations offering aid were members and, after all, this was a military, not a civilian matter. Better still, confidential talks could be held at NATO headquarters in Belgium. That would minimize leaks to the Russian press.

A delegation was dispatched to Brussels.

Even with this tactic, the high command faced a sharp reality. If they were able to quickly get inside the sunken submarine, all offers of assistance would be moot. Speed was the key. Every hour that passed without gaining entry pushed them closer to the point where refusing to accept aid would place them in a bad public light.

The rescue operation now took on a dual personality. Those leading the effort possessed information about the extent of the damage to the *Kursk*. These officials therefore had a better understanding of the possibility of finding anyone alive. The Navy was also committed to a path of action. The foreign sub story, in one form or another, caused the least problems and protected the most careers. The officials really wanted to sell it any, and every, way it could be sold. For this elite group, an end to news media coverage and public outcries could not come soon enough.

The many seamen who were actually participating in the operation considered themselves in a race with death to save the lives of the *Kursk* crew. Performing dangerous tasks at a frantic pace, these were the individuals whose unquestioned bravery and devotion to duty were inspirational. Focusing the news media on their courageous efforts helped shift media attention away from the cause of the crash.

1600 Hours—Rescue Site

The order to bring in the newer model Russian DSRV caused several problems. First was the matter of getting it from port to the *Kursk*'s resting place. The submersible *AS-36* Bester model had no mother ship. Its support vessel, the *Herman Titov*, had been taken out of operation in 1994. Since *AS-36* could not reach the rescue area under its own power, transportation was needed.

A floating crane was commandeered. It lifted the 40-foot-long minisub into the air. To stop it from swinging because of wave motion, lines were used to secure the bow and stern. One of the Northern Fleet rescue tugs then towed the crane and submersible to the recovery spot. By this point several other support ships had arrived as well, so there was now a small flotilla at the scene.

On-site the weather had turned, making for rougher seas. The floating crane, designed for port and coastal tasks, became difficult to manage in the offshore waves. When the submersible began swaying violently, the men realized something had to be done quickly or the rescue vehicle would be seriously damaged. It was decided that unloading the DSRV into the now-turbulent water without banging it up was impossible.

A tugboat moved into position and pushed the crane and *AS-36* toward Porchnikha, the nearest bay. Once there, they found calmer seas. Improvising, a crew managed to control the worst of the DSRV's gyrations. Working slowly because of danger from the swinging mass, they got the boat into the water. They then struggled to free it from the crane. The tug pulled alongside the boat, a line was secured, and at a sedate pace, *AS-36* was towed back for use.

The three-man crew boarded the submersible and took their stations. It was decided that a trial dive to check all systems was best. The DSRV submerged and its controls were tested. There was some damage but she seemed to respond adequately. After resurfacing briefly, they went down again.

AS-36 held a good sonar fix on the *Kursk* and started to close on the boat. Intent on this maneuver, no one noticed the slight drip of hydraulic fluid from a pipe. The drip grew to a trickle, then quickly into a thin jet of flammable red liquid spewing across the inside of the crew compartment. A valve that helps regulate controls for the boat's trim had sprung a leak. If it were not capped, and quickly, it would drain all the fluid, rendering the controls useless. At this depth, if the entire fitting failed, there was a strong probability that pressure would force water into the rescue vehicle.

Radio contact with the surface was maintained while the crew attempted to deal with the problem. Finding they couldn't stop the leak and were in fact experiencing control difficulties, they took decisive action.

As gently as possible, they allowed the boat to settle into the ooze and muck of the sea floor. Clouds of silt were billowed by their slowly turning prop. They deliberately grounded themselves. On the bottom, no controls were needed to maintain direction or depth. This allowed them to place the boat's rudder and all diving planes in a neutral position, which lowered hydraulic pressure in the system, slowing fluid loss. If they could not repair the leak, their only option was to blow all ballast and make a dangerous blind emergency ascent. The crew of the *Kursk* had tried this same trick. For them, it had been too late.

The maneuver was risky enough in open ocean where traffic is light. In the disaster area, though, there were some 20-plus ships, tugs, and units of floating equipment. Rushing to the surface and popping up underneath another vessel would be deadly. The continued loss of hydraulic fluid presented another crisis. If they reached daylight, they would be unable to steer. So they risked ramming a ship.

It took only a few moments to realize that making a repair with the tools and materials on board was impossible. If anything, the leak was worse.

They had two safety measures. First, they could do a semiaccurate sonar scan of the water above them. That would tell them if the area directly overhead was unobstructed at the time they started up. Undersea currents would shift their position as they rose, so it might not be clear when they got there, but it would at least be open ocean when they started.

The other advantage was their emergency homing beacon. With it turned on, the *Rudnitsky* would have a tight fix on them. Other vessels could be warned away from the surfacing zone. Then the *Rudnitsky* could run in quickly to pick them up.

They discussed the plan by radio, and since no one had a better idea, *AS-36* received permission to perform the sudden ballast release once the area had been evacuated.

Sitting in the silence of the deep, the crew shut down all electrical drains. They had no choice. They needed maximum battery power to control the release of compressed air into the water ballast tanks. With heaters cut off, cold began to seep in, even though the hull was insulated. The wait gave the men an opportunity to think about their fellow submariners in the *Kursk*. For this moment, they shared a common fate with those they were risking their lives to rescue. There was a single, vital difference, however. *AS-36* still had one last means of escape from the depths.

The radio crackled. They were to go for emergency ascent.

There was a pause, then the outrush of water created a geyser of bubbles and sea floor slime. AS-36 surged through this curtain, accelerating rapidly. As they shot toward the surface, the sea around them turned from black to deep blue, to a lighter aqua.

The pickup crew on the *Rudnitsky* knew where to watch for *AS-36*. The massive eruption of bubbles gave ample warning of its arrival. Breaking out of the cold water with a loud splash, the craft shot over half its length into the clean air, then dropped, creating a sharp series of waves.

Inside the minisub there was relieved cheering as they broke the surface, then grunts as the nose slammed flat into the sea. In an orderly fashion, they went through the shutdown procedure. With the controls gone, the motor was useless.

Next, they opened the watertight hatch. Daylight and fresh air flooded in, lessening the petroleum reek of the spilled hydraulic fluid.

A tug drew alongside, bobbing in the waves. The men scrabbled over the slick, still dripping metal plates of the submersible's hull. A sailor threw a heavy line. It was caught and quickly made fast to a towing cleat.

The diesel engine on the tug roared, throwing black smoke into the sky. The rope line tensioned, rising out of the water as the slack was taken up. They were under way.

Then *AS-36* swerved crazily. The crew on the sloping deck was almost knocked off their feet. They recognized the trouble at once. With the hydraulic fluid gone, there was no pressure on the rudder and diving planes to hold them in a set position. As the minisub began to make headway, water acted on each control surface differently, sending the boat into wild gyrations. The rolling was strong enough to cause water to splash through the open hatch.

The unchecked pitching of its captive at the other end of the line jerked the stern of the tug this way and that. One moment the boxy transom would rise out of the sea until the turning prop was visible, then violently snap down and veer off to one side. Next, and at random, she'd swing back hard enough to make the hull shudder with the strain of being turned.

The submersible's crew had no option but to hang on and hope they didn't take in enough water to sink them.

Skillful handling of the tug brought *AS-36* as close to the *Rudnitsky* as possible. Timing one erratic swing just right, the tugboat reversed engines, slacking the tow rope. An instant later, the line was cast free, allowing inertia to send the small sub alongside its tender.

A crane was already lowering a lift cradle from the deck above. Men secured *AS-36* just before she floundered, saving the vessel, which was hoisted aboard for repairs.

In spite of Navy Press Office efforts to hold back the flood of public attention, time was running out.

On Monday, August 14, no word about the massive rescue operation had been officially released by the Navy. On August 15, three days after the accident, news stories cited the Navy as being ready to move into the "active phase." The various descents of the DSRVs on Tuesday and Wednesday, August 15 through 16, would be called the "first" and "second" attempts, in an effort to give the impression that activity had just begun.

Additional accounts compounded the confusion. The RIA news agency quoted a Northern Fleet Headquarters press officer as saying the crew was not in danger and the process of abandoning the sub had not been raised. Interfax, another news service, cited a source as stating it was "not excluded" there were casualties. Interfax also noted sources in Murmansk indicating a rescue diving bell had been lowered to the *Kursk* and was supplying the submarine with oxygen, fuel, and air for its ballast chambers. Other news services had stories of "acoustic contact" with those on the stricken boat. *Itar-Tass* apparently named Navy Chief Admiral Vladimir Kuroyedov as revealing that the chances for a positive outcome were not very high. He also was quoted as saying the *Kursk* looked as if it had suffered from some kind of collision. Another item in *The Moscow Times* was attributed to a Northern Fleet spokesman who is said to have reported by telephone from the Navy base at Severomorsk: "We have learnt through tapping that there are no dead among the *Kursk* crew, but it remains unknown whether there are casualties."

The need to gain entry into the sub, accept foreign assistance, or face public disapproval, which would make the damage-due-to-collision story less effective, was now a pressing issue. It had to be resolved. Understandably, efforts to get inside the *Kursk* became even more intense.

CHAPTER 7

15 August 2000—Barents Sea

ACTIVITY AT THE *KURSK* SITE, ALREADY ON THE NAVY'S sea-duty, nonstop, 24-hour-a-day schedule, became hectic. Men willingly gave up free time to perform double shifts. Laboring in this northern place, where the cold summer sun shines at night, they lost track of time. There was no morning, noon, or evening. There was only work that proceeded on several fronts at an increasingly frantic pace. A large part of the effort, however, was based on trial and error. Prior experience in actual hands-on undersea rescue was limited—because, considering the length of time modern nuclear submarines spend submerged, disasters seldom occur.

Since the first nuclear submarine, *Nautilus*, was launched by the U.S. in 1954, the list of sinkings and serious onboard fires is surprisingly short.

On April 10, 1963, an American attack submarine, the USS *Thresher*, made a test dive in the Atlantic, east of

Boston, Massachusetts. She never resurfaced. All 129 on board perished.

In September 1967, 39 Soviet crewmen died from a fire on their November-class submarine in the Norwegian Sea. The boat managed to surface, which saved the rest.

In May of 1968, a nuclear reactor malfunction aboard the Soviet *K-27* spread radiation through the sub. The vessel was so contaminated it was dumped into the Kara Sea in 1981.

On May 22, 1968, the USS *Scorpion* went down in open ocean southwest of the Azores. A torpedo mishap was named the likely cause. Ninety-nine men were lost.

Sometime during 1968, an unnamed Soviet submarine sank while operating inside the Arctic Circle.

During April 1970, fires broke out in the interior of a submerged Soviet November-class sub in the Bay of Biscay, forcing it to the surface. The intense blaze burned for three days and sank the boat. Fifty-two of the crew died.

In February 1972, a Soviet Hotel-class vessel had a hydraulic line failure and fire. At the cost of 28 lives, the crew fought the blaze for 24 days before being rescued.

On August 21, 1980, an Echo-1-class Soviet submarine surfaced off the coast of Japan. Nine died because of radiation leaks and fire.

In the summer of 1983, an unnamed Soviet submarine in the North Pacific went to the bottom with 90 men.

In 1986, some 600 miles east of Bermuda, a Yankee-class Soviet missile sub sank after an onboard explosion. Four of the crew met death.

On April 7, 1989, a Soviet attack submarine, the *Kom-*

somolets, suffered a fire and sank in the Norwegian Sea. Forty-two of the crew of 69 perished.

That's a total of 12 incidents, including the *Kursk*, during a period of more than 46 years. Less serious fires on U.S. boats have occurred. Other Russian sinkings may also have happened. If so, these accidents are still classified. The Russian newspaper *Izvestia* reportedly accounted for 507 missing submariners in the Russian Navy during the past 40 years. This number makes it likely that not all of their large episodes have been made public.

Only two of the sunken nuclear-powered submarines listed above were American. Loss of the *Thresher* in 1963 brought about the SUBSAFE program, instituted by the U.S. Navy. From the revamping of fire suppression drills to the installation of flame-resistant materials where possible, to more exacting specifications for even minor fittings on the boat, every aspect of the submarine and its operations was scrutinized. This rigorous policy focused on reducing the danger inherent in undersea activities. Standards tightened even more after the 1968 *Scorpion* disaster. Both these tragedies received worldwide attention in the news media.

Until the *Kursk*, news coverage of Soviet submarine casualties came only when it was impossible to keep the incident quiet. The 1989 *Komsomolets* fire and sinking, for example, was publicized because its location was close to Norway.

Under the Soviet regime, the downing of a submarine, or for that matter any naval catastrophe, was a classified matter.

At this point in the *Kursk* tragedy, secrecy of another

sort was playing a role. No one knew for certain how many of the crew, if any, trapped aboard the *Kursk* were still alive. A damage assessment was not publicly released. Had it been, hopes would not have been high. Knowledge of an onboard explosion was spreading. So a number of deaths was generally anticipated although most still believed there were survivors. Based on previous sub accidents, rescuing at least some of the crew was a possibility—even long after reason dictated giving up hope.

In 1983, for instance, a highly professional and courageous Russian officer on a sunken submarine maintained his command of the situation and helped hold his men together for three weeks.

And as long ago as 1939, the men aboard the USS *Squalus*, which sank in 260 feet of water, waited 36 hours before help arrived. Twenty-six submariners died. The remaining 30 were saved when a diving bell was lowered and attached to the sub's hatch. Then, three or four at a time, the crew climbed into the bell, resealed the hatch, and the bell with its cargo was brought to the surface.

As part of the disaster rescue efforts, the Russians were unsuccessfully using diving bells from the *Altay* to duplicate the *Squalus* process. Problems rescuers encountered were attributed to swift undersea currents and hatch damage, the same difficulties that stymied the submersibles.

Recovery Site

By 0800 hours, waves in the Barents Sea were rising to 13 feet and the rescue ships were slammed by 45-mile-

The Russian nuclear submarine *Kursk* at a naval base in Vidyaevo in May 2000. (AP/WORLD WIDE PHOTOS)

Captain-Lieutenant Dmitry Kolesnikov and his wife, Olga, in front of the conning tower or sail of the *Kursk*, while the boat is docked at the Severomorsk naval base. Dmitry and Olga were married on April 28, 2000, just a few months before the tragic sinking. (AFP)

On board the *Kursk* a few months before the sinking, crew-members man their stations. (AP/WORLD WIDE PHOTOS)

Captain Gennadi Lyachin, commander of the *Kursk,* in front of the submarine at the naval base in Vidyaevo, during October 1999. Lyachin was posthumously awarded one of Russia's highest honors by President Vladimir Putin.

(AP/WORLD WIDE PHOTOS)

Vyacheslav Popov, commander of the Russian Northern Fleet, aboard the *Admiral Chabanenko*, during the October 2000 undersea operations to enter the sunken *Kursk*.
(AP/WORLD WIDE PHOTOS)

The Russian nuclear-powered *Peter the Great* and a service vessel at anchor near the site where the *Kursk* went down. This image was made from a television report on August 18, 2000. (AP/WORLD WIDE PHOTOS)

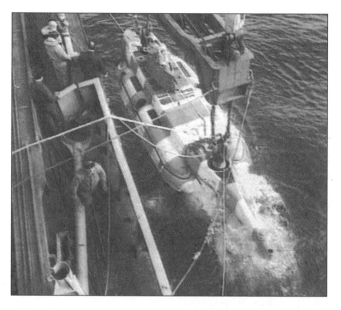

A Russian Deep Sea Rescue Vehicle is lowered from the side of its tender ship, the *Rudnitsky,* on Friday, August 18, 2000, after a frantic race to reach the site of the sunken *Kursk.* (AP/WORLD WIDE PHOTOS)

Russian President Vladimir Putin, on the left, confers with Deputy Prime Minister Ilya Klebanov (center) and head of the Russian Navy, Admiral Kuroyedov on August 22, 2000, prior to a meeting with the lost submariners' families. (AP/ WORLD WIDE PHOTOS)

An immense platform ship, the *Regalia,* stationed at the *Kursk* recovery site on Sunday, October 22, 2000. The *Regalia* provided accommodations for divers and other personnel during the recovery effort. (AP/WORLD WIDE PHOTOS)

A mourning ceremony held at Severomorsk, homeport of the *Kursk*, was held on Sunday, October 29, 2000. Caskets containing the remains of four of the crew were placed atop military vehicles for the sad procession. (AP/WORLD WIDE PHOTOS)

per-hour winds. It was anticipated that gale conditions would worsen before improving. So all undersea operations were curtailed. Hundreds of men, anxious to help their comrades, were forced to wait.

At 0900 hours, the Navy released a statement indicating the crew on board the *Kursk* was tapping on the hull. This news flashed through the rescue flotilla. Sitting idle now became even more difficult and stressful.

Other press reports were continuing. Russian officers were at NATO headquarters holding a conference on available assistance. The British began prepping their *LR-5* rescue sub for action. The Russian Navy maintained it could handle the rescue unaided. A report from Norwegian sources claimed the Russians had given notice of the accident to their foreign office on Saturday, August 12, rather than Sunday. The *Kursk*'s designer reportedly took full responsibility for the accident. "Something extraordinary, beyond the imagination of an engineer," had happened.

Navy Chief Admiral Vladimir Kuroyedov was informed that oxygen reserves on board the *Kursk* would last until noon on Friday, August 18. A leak to Reuters News Service declared that oxygen on board the *Kursk* was running low. One story seemed to breed another. Fancy became repeated fact. And facts changed as they appeared in the next story.

Navy scuttlebutt channels were full of rumors as well. Some, sadly, proved to be true. Families of the crew members at the Northern Fleet's sub bases near Murmansk somehow received unofficial word that there was no hope for survivors. As might be imagined, this news caused emotional turmoil. To contain the situation and control information flow, the bases were sealed. The already-monitored telephone lines were temporarily placed out of order.

As hours passed, the storm at the recovery site had grown more ferocious. Then, late on August 15 at about 2000 hours, there came a break.

Braving wet decks in wind-driven rain, Navy men deployed the DSRVs. During the next nine hours, four separate attempts were made to dock with the submarine's rear escape hatch. All failed. The same problems experienced earlier still prevailed. The current was too strong, the angle of the sub to the sea floor was too great, visibility was poor, and damaged mating surfaces on the hatch prevented the rescuers from making a watertight connection. As the weather showed signs of worsening, meetings were called to regroup forces and plan the next steps.

Those in the know realized this well might be the final effort before requesting foreign assistance. If they failed to achieve entry into the sub during the next few hours, public pressure to do so would become unmanageable. Recriminations for not acting sooner would be more difficult to explain. Like it or not, the need to accept Western help, no matter how embarrassing that might be, was becoming imperative.

16 August 2000—0800 Hours—Barents Sea

The fourth day dawned with a prediction of more storms. While that was disappointing, spirits rose with the arrival of another DSRV. This was a welcome addition to the fleet because the reliable *AS-34* needed to be removed from the water and swung aboard the *Rudnitsky* for essential maintenance tasks. Repairs would enable the sub to be used for a longer period when placed back into service.

Crane lines were made fast to *AS-34*. As she was lifted from the sea she swung in the wind, violently slamming her hull into the ship. Men grabbed cables dangling from the boat and struggled to stabilize the DSRV before the minisub hit again. It was too late. The damage had been done.

A quick inspection revealed antennas required for sonar and electronic sensing had been broken. There were no replacements. Fixes were improvised and the submersible was able to return to limited service.

While rushed repairs were being made to *AS-34*, other plans were evaluated. One concept was to lay water-filled pontoons alongside the *Kursk* hull. These floats would be connected by web belts. Compressed air could then be piped into the cylinders, forcing the water out. The pontoons would rise and lift the giant boat to the surface. The procedure was ruled more a salvage operation than a crew-rescue program, so the idea was discarded.

Another concept called for connecting electrical power cables and an oxygen hose to the submarine. As there were no connectors on the *Kursk*'s hull suitable for such use, the necessary hardware would have to be fabricated and then attached by divers. The length of time required to accomplish this ruled out the project.

By this point, different types of Deep Sea Rescue Vehicles had made more than ten attempts to dock and connect with the rear escape hatch. All had failed. The DSRV crews were willing to continue. There was little hope, however, that they would be able to perform a successful rescue. Even so, these men were the most effective option the Russian Navy possessed.

Rumors sprang from failures. One held that the *Kursk* lay on the bottom with a 60-degree list and her bow down at an angle of 20 degrees. This position, tail high and leaning to one side, coupled with a swift current over the hull, suggested the need for help.

At 1500 hours, President Vladimir Putin, still on holiday in the Black Sea resort of Sochi, described the situation as "critical."

Shortly afterward, Deputy Prime Minister Ilya Klebanov was quoted as saying there were no signs of life on the sub—this despite recent reports of hammering on the inside of the hull.

Four days had elapsed. It was time for a different approach. After due consultation, President Putin, acting in his capacity as supreme commander-in-chief, passed the order for Navy head Admiral Vladimir Kuroyedov to accept foreign assistance. Kuroyedov's team acted immediately to arrange help from both Britain and Norway.

This presidential action was a political masterstroke. Being ordered to accept outside aid allowed the Navy to continue its effort while negotiations for help were under way. If Russia succeeded in entering the sub, national pride would be even greater. If they failed, they had still asked for assistance. The talks would overcome any future complaints about an unwillingness to look outside Russia for aid. Acting under orders also allowed the Navy to accept assistance without having to admit an inability to perform the needed tasks.

Russia formally requested that Britain lend the *LR-5*

minisubmarine and crew. The British had readied the rescue vessel in case it was needed and approval to airlift the *LR-5* into Norway was instantly granted. At 1900 hours, a transport carrying the *LR-5* landed at the naval and port city of Trondheim.

At 1200 hours on August 16, the Northern Fleet chief of staff called the commander of the Norwegian Navy on their direct line to request assistance on behalf of Admiral Popov.

The Norwegians were asked to help in three different ways. First, alterations to the *LR-5* hatch were essential so a watertight seal could be made with the *Kursk*. According to reports, a Norwegian manufacturing facility in Kirkeness was selected for this project. Next, transportation for the British *LR-5* was needed from Norway's Trondheim Navy Base to the rescue site. And finally, divers capable of working at depths exceeding 300 feet, along with their support vessel and necessary gear, were required.

The Russian Navy's diving school had been closed by lack of funding but they still had capable divers. Several volunteered their skills for the rescue effort. What the Russians lacked was the specialized equipment required for working long periods underwater to open the *Kursk* hatches. The rescue gear used for saturation diving had been rented out to oil companies.

Saturation diving was perfected by the U.S. Navy during the late 1950s. Since that time the practice has spread from the military into civilian commercial and scientific applications. Offshore oil exploration and production industries, in particular, employ many saturation divers. This type of diving is the only method for a person to work underwater at depths as great as 2,000 feet without a lengthy decompression period.

To handle the Russian request for divers, six employees of Stolt Offshore, a Norwegian contractor to the oil and gas industry, were pulled from a job near Haltenbanken, Norway. The four Britons and two Norwegians were aboard Stolt-Comex's diving ship, *Seaway Eagle*, based out of Aberdeen, Scotland. Eight hours after the Russian call for aid, the team was rushing to the accident site.

At 1200 hours on August 17, a Norwegian vessel, the *Normand Pioneer*, had loaded the British *LR-5* and departed from the port of Trondheim.

By this point, political storm flags were snapping in the wind. Public outcries caused the Russian government to form a special commission for overseeing rescue operations and investigating causes of the accident. Deputy Prime Minister Ilya Klebanov was named chairman of this group.

17 August 2000

Five days had passed since the accident and despite many tries, there had been no entry into the *Kursk*. All talk about tapping on the hull was done. The earlier stories now appeared to be just that—stories. Specialists, reviewing audiotapes of the tapping sounds, detected no Morse code. Some experts now believed the noises were caused by popping metal as the *Kursk* settled into the seafloor sediment.

Underwater surveys of the boat had been expanded and the extent of damage to the submarine was now better understood. It was difficult for experienced Navy officers to hold much hope. Admitting a lost cause would bring unwanted reactions and dangerous questions. So silence on the true state of affairs continued—the same silence that helped maintain a state of anxiety.

Prime Minister Mikhail Kasyanov, the number two man in Russian government, was quoted in *The St. Petersburg Times* as saying the situation was "close to catastrophic." At almost the same instant, the Navy Press Center announced that those on board could survive until August 23, possibly August 25, if they were careful with air and water supplies.

Whether or not anyone lived inside the wreckage, foreign help was on the way. And at least some of the Russians resented the intrusion of foreigners into their work. This reaction caused yet another redoubling of Russian rescue efforts. If there was any possible way, Navy personnel were determined to gain entry into the *Kursk* before "help" reached the site.

A fourth DSRV arrived and was quickly readied. With added support, a renewed series of attempts to dock with the submarine began immediately. The previous problems remained and were cited as reasons for repeated failures.

At the same time this grueling undersea struggle was taking place, better news was found. Water samples taken near the wreck and at random locations in the area continued to show no traces of unusual radiation levels. As hoped, the nuclear piles had automatically shut down. This information was especially important to the Norwegians, who were invited to take their own samples. The Barents Sea, despite this and other dumped reactors, remains one of the least radioactively polluted bodies of water in the world.

To lend air support to the rescue flotilla, the heavy aircraft-carrying cruiser *Admiral Flota Sovetskogo Soyuza Kuznetsov* was brought within 15 miles of the site. This additional resource provided air cover that allowed for increasing helicopter patrols seeking foreign subs that might be lurking in the zone.

On the political front, Russian military delegates continued to meet with NATO officials. And a new voice was heard on the collision theory. Admiral Eduard Baltin, a senior commander of submarine operations in the old Soviet Pacific Fleet, came forward with a statement during an interview. He was quoted as saying, "I think the only realistic version is that the sub collided with a cargo vessel because it is in an area where there is a recommenced course for civil navigation."

If the foreign sub story failed to hold, any collision would apparently do.

On this same day, Russian officials reported that George Tenet, director of the U.S. Central Intelligence Agency, arrived in Moscow for talks. Some part of those conversations most likely touched on the *Kursk* situation. While there was speculation as to the cause of Tenet's visit, several newspapers reported that this meeting had been arranged before the *Kursk* disaster. The CIA and FSB, the Russian Federal Security Service, periodically discuss such issues as terrorism, drug trafficking, and organized crime.

At the same time, the Government *Kursk* Inquiry Commission, headed by Deputy Prime Minister Ilya Klebanov, was meeting at the Severomorsk headquarters of the Northern Fleet. Ranking officers convened for eight hours to decide whether or not to continue their rescue operation. The committee also considered possible explanations for the disaster. Klebanov leaned toward a collision as the primary cause. The group also announced further study of a plan to raise the *Kursk* and remove its two nuclear reactors.

Other theories, once quietly espoused, now began to leak to the news media. The *Kursk* might have struck a World War II mine. Or a sudden release of chlorine gas, a product of the batteries on board, could have knocked the crew unconscious. The list of possible causes grew longer. It would soon include terrorist action by Chechen rebel forces. Eventually the possibility of a UFO action, an act of God, or curse of the devil were considered. Any reason that cast no blame held an attraction.

18 August 2000

On the morning of August 18, six days after the accident, a single headline indicated control of the news media had slipped away. The Murmansk edition of the popular newspaper, *Komsomolskaya Pravda*, played it big: "18,000 Rubles for the Names of the Sailors of the *Kursk*."

Readers were informed that due to repeated refusals by the Northern Fleet and the Navy to supply a list of the *Kursk* crew, the paper had acted. They paid a "high ranking Moscow naval officer" the sum of 18,000 rubles (about $645) for a list stamped "Top Secret" by Navy commanders.

The Russian media had been pressuring officials for a

crew list. The response had been negative because, according to the Navy, relatives of those on board had been informed privately. There was no need for a public posting.

Vladimir Shkoda, editor of the Murmansk edition, disagreed. He felt that publication of the list would offer reassurance to many families that their son or husband was not among the missing. According to his statement, the paper had tried unsuccessfully for three days to obtain the list. It was important to tell the families the names of those fighting for survival out there and just who was tapping the SOS on the inside of the hull. Disclosing the full list would keep many from worrying needlessly.

Publication of the roster over the objections of the Navy, and the manner in which the list was acquired, came as a sharp blow to officials attempting to manage the press. And, since no one likes to be scooped, the release was a prod to the other news media to go after stories any way they could. It was also an opportunity for the media with a political agenda to use the disaster as a means of attacking President Putin.

The first salvo in this discredit-Putin game was fired by painting him as uncaring because he did not leave his vacation and immediately rush to the disaster site. There had been murmurs of discontent along that line for the past few days. Now they became angry rumblings that refused to subside.

To deal with the assault, Putin attempted a direct approach. In a newspaper account of a TV interview he gave from the city of Yalta, Putin was said to have appeared calm. He'd traveled to that resort for a summit of representatives from former Soviet republics. During the interview he reportedly explained that when Defense Minister Igor Sergeyev had informed him of the disaster he asked about the crew's chances. The response he'd received was that there was a very small hope for rescue, but that it was still a possibility.

He also noted he had not gone to the scene because he felt his presence would only hamper the rescue efforts. "Everyone should keep to his place," was his reply.

Putin's remarks, although well received by most people, did little to stop his "lack of concern" from being played again and again by certain news sources. Open accusations of other authorities neglecting their duties soon followed. And headlines became vicious: "Putin Robs 118 Men of Four Days." The story also contained accusatory comments: "By hiding in sunny Sochi, Putin has disappointed many who thought he would be a different sort of leader . . ." and ". . . then those deaths can be directly attributed to the president's arrogance."

Commander of Russia's Northern Fleet, Admiral Vyacheslav Popov, also chose August 18 to make his first public statement since the accident. Looking grave and obviously weary, he insisted that all the fleet's work had been directed toward saving the crew. He had special praise for the operators of the DSRVs, noting that they were extremely tired but were not going to quit.

In an open admission, Popov discussed flooding aboard the *Kursk*. He raised the problem of incoming water compressing trapped air, thus increasing air pressure on board. This process, he explained, negated the validity of previous estimates concerning how long breathable air inside the submarine would last.

In the same interview, he attempted to reconcile the now-released Norwegian seismograph readings, which were evidence of an explosion, with the official commission theory of a collision with a foreign sub. In a new spin, he said, "There was an explosion inside a compartment of the submarine, but the reason for the blast could be because of something from the outside, I mean a collision, or . . ." He did not mention that "something from the outside" might have been a missile.

Shortly, the official line would be a collision caused the *Kursk* to sink, and impact with the bottom set off the explosions.

To help contradict the collision notion, the USS *Memphis*, one of the American subs that had been observing the Russian sea games, arrived in Norway. On a scheduled stop for crew leave, the boat docked at the Haakonsvern Navy Base outside the city of Bergen.

There was no effort by the American government to deny that the *Memphis* had been in the proximity of the sunken *Kursk*. The earliest reports of the accident made mention of the U.S. submarines. Four Russian Ilyushin-38 surveillance aircraft, following a submarine, almost breeched Norwegian airspace. Two Norwegian fighter jets were scrambled in response. Then the next day, August 18, two more of the IL-38s repeated the near intrusion. These planes were following what the Russians claim to have been the *Memphis*.

As a precaution, Admiral Einar Skorgen contacted Admiral Popov to discover why the Russian planes had almost violated Norwegian airspace. He was told there had been a collision with the *Kursk* and the planes had been searching for the submarine involved.

When the *Memphis* docked, an alert U.S. Embassy obtained clearance and quickly staged a photo opportunity. Russian photographers were pointedly invited to participate. The offer was instantly accepted and all photos of the submarine showed no damage. This session did little to set aside the collision concept, but the shots later served to counter a deliberate Russian trick using satellite photos.

17–18 August 2000—Disaster Site

Crews on the various Russian ships watched as Norwegian helicopters zoomed in low and hovered while taking water samples. Testing for radioactivity in air and sea was now being performed frequently by both nations. Results, to everyone's relief, continued to indicate no contamination.

Russian Deep Sea Rescue Vehicles were diving in rotation. One submerged, attempted as many dockings with the *Kursk* as possible, and resurfaced. Then another took its place and began its series of tries. This pattern gave the men little rest. They were near exhaustion from their intensive schedules.

Finally, on one attempt, a crew met with success. They docked and managed to lock into the emergency hatch. Following procedures carefully, they achieved a partial seal with the hatch. The next maneuver was to pump water from the escape tube under the hatch before opening it. They tried, then tried again, all the while talking with their control officer on the ship above them. With battery power and air running low, they cast off from the *Kursk* and returned to the surface.

With a crew heartened by the successful docking, the next DSRV sank beneath the now-shallow waves. They managed to dock as well but were equally frustrated by an inability to drain the escape route that would allow the hatch to open. This tense, difficult, unending routine was repeated over and over. Yet the hatch remained closed.

Engineers gathered with the DSRV crew members to view videotapes and discuss the difficulties. No one liked either of the two conclusions finally agreed upon.

It was decided that impact with the sea bottom distorted the hatch enough to prevent forming an acceptable seal between the DSRV and the hatch coaming. This lack of a seal made draining the escape route impossible.

Or, and this was a thought that gave everyone present a sense of horror, one of the men trapped inside the *Kursk* had attempted an escape through the hatch. The tube had become depressurized and was now flooded. The body of that hapless submariner might still be in the chute.

The use of divers presented the best solution to these problems. Equipped with the right tools, a team could open the hatch and check the escape chute. Divers, however, could not bring up survivors.

So it was agreed that further DSRV attempts should continue. Expectations were not high. There was only one bitter, but practical, alternative. They could stop operations and await the arrival of foreign assistance.

These were courageous men, with powerful spirits, strong pride in country, belief in their Navy, and an unquenchable will to win. They refused to sit and do nothing.

CHAPTER 8

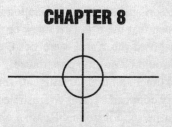

18 August 2000—Aboard the Normand Pioneer

THE NORWEGIAN AND BRITISH TEAMS THAT RACED TOWARD
the disaster site were strongly united by their mission to
save lives. And they were rapidly approaching the unofficial "stay alive for seven days" rule for submariners
trapped in the deep. The 21 engineers, doctors, and rescuers on board the *Normand Pioneer* were scheduled to
arrive at 1800 hours the next day. The divers on *Seaway
Eagle* would be on station five hours later. When they got
to the site, they wanted to be ready to begin operations.
So they asked the Russians for information and meetings
on board the *Normand Pioneer* while en route. The Russians demurred.

A Royal Navy officer, Commodore David Russell,
was the scene-of-action commander for the British diving
team. Norwegian Vice Admiral Skorgen personally led
the Norwegian contingent. Neither man wanted to be idle

during the journey. If the data requested was provided, the transit period could be used to better prepare.

The Russians, possibly to give their comrades more time to gain entry into the *Kursk* on their own, wished to hold off technical discussions and planning until the foreigners arrived on-site. Another explanation for this delay might have been that the Russians knew or strongly suspected all on board the *Kursk* were dead, and one day more or less would be of little importance.

Admiral Skorgen, a highly intelligent, very direct, effective military commander, was so frustrated by Russian resistance that he set a deadline. Russian experts would meet with his people, the LR-5 team, and the divers no later than August 19.

Late on August 18, the Russians finally gave their approval. A team was flown to an airfield in Vardoe, Norway. There, they boarded a Norwegian GKN-Westland Sea King rescue helicopter and were transported to the *Seaway Eagle*. Their arrival set the stage for the first trilateral technical assistance meeting the next morning.

Rescue Site

Even though work by the crews manning the Deep Sea Rescue Vehicles had been curtailed by the engineering report, they wanted to continue. As long as there was even the slightest chance of making a sealed, watertight docking, they were willing to try. Every trip to the bottom was life threatening, but they accepted that risk.

The first DSRV was down almost two grueling hours. Finding the sub was no longer a problem. Little time was wasted in transit, which allowed several docking attempts to be made on each trip.

Nearing exhaustion, rescue workers had deteriorated reflexes. Moving cautiously through the darkness, inching along the outer hull, struggling not to overcontrol, trying to keep the DSRV stable and lined up with the hatch—all were taxing and frustrating. The men continued, however, diving again and again, operating on nerve and pride.

19 August 2000—Aboard the Normand Pioneer

The Russian-Norwegian-British technical conference went well enough. A plan for the diving routine was developed, modified, and approved—with one small omission. No specific time for the divers to start was established. There were conflicting reports about bottom conditions and the sub's angle of rest. And if the worst were true, divers would find it almost impossible to work.

By 1930 hours, the *Normand Pioneer* and the *Seaway Eagle* had the flotilla in sight. Then the spirit of that morning's cooperation waned.

Both ships were ordered to stop and hold their positions. When asked why, the Russians replied that they wanted time for their DSRVs to make two more docking attempts. If these failed, they would utilize the deep-sea divers. When would the final Russian effort end? Sometime on August 20, the next day.

Admiral Skorgen had a different concept of his mission. He was quoted as saying, "That has irritated me a little bit, that we have to accept to wait. But this is the fact, this is a Russian operation. We are supporting them and have to accept it."

Even so, he instantly argued against any delay. Skorgen pointed out that his intention, and that of his team, was to save lives. Playing the role of a passive observer was out of the question. After some debate, a compromise was reached. The *Seaway Eagle* was allowed to proceed to its diving station. The *Normand Pioneer*, with its cargo of the British *LR-5*, was to remain some 20 nautical miles away. At least the divers, who had been prepping themselves, would be in a position to perform the work they had been brought in to do.

Using newly installed satellite navigation gear, the *Seaway Eagle* positioned itself above the wreckage. Once she was in place, computers were locked on to the location by satellite fix. As the ship, displaced by currents, waves, and swells, drifted off station even the slightest amount, sensors detected the change. Electronically, computers started and stopped enormous underwater propellers, called "thrusters," that maneuvered the ship in any desired direction. This constant relocation allowed the vessel to hover in the water over an exact spot without anchoring. While "dynamic positioning" was being established, the divers were completing the time required to acclimate themselves to the depth at which they were to work.

Saturation diving requires highly skilled, well-trained men, a special ship with pressurized living quarters, and time to "saturate" the divers.

As a diver goes deeper, external pressure on his body increases because the weight of water is greater than that of air. For normal breathing, air must be supplied to the diver's lungs at a pressure about equal to that around the diver's body.

Breathing air at higher and higher pressure causes some of the inert gases, notably nitrogen, to dissolve into the diver's body. If the diver surfaces too quickly, the dissolved gas will form bubbles in the tissues and bloodstream. These bubbles cause acute pain and can be fatal. This condition is known as decompression sickness. If the bubbles form in the body's joints, the diver "bends" in pain, hence the common name "bends." The bubbles may cause dizziness, blindness, hearing problems, loss of consciousness, and even result in death.

The process of releasing pressure can be compared to opening a bottle of champagne. Pop the cork off suddenly and you expose the bottle's contents to normal air pressure. The gas dissolved in the liquid suddenly is freed from the solution. Hence the familiar foaming overflow.

If the champagne cork is removed slowly over a period of hours, allowing the pressure inside the bottle to gradually equal outside pressure, the gas escapes without forming bubbles. What's left is an expensive, "flat" white wine.

A diver must do much the same with his body. To avoid the bends while surfacing, a diver has to slowly lower the amount of pressure on the tissues to finally equal that of the surface. This process, known as "decompression," requires time. In general, the deeper the dive and the longer the period at depth, the longer the time needed to decompress. Staying only 15 minutes at a relatively shallow 260 feet requires several hours' decompression. That's a short work span for a lengthy return to normal atmospheric pressure.

To overcome such long recovery periods, saturation divers enter a living chamber or habitat aboard the mother ship. Pressure inside the chamber is gradually raised to equal the pressure underwater at which the divers will work. In the chamber, they begin to breathe a mixture of oxygen and inert gas, such as helium or helium and nitrogen. As their bodies acclimate to the increasing pressure and breathing mix, their blood and tissues become permeated with the gas they inhale. After about 12 hours, the tissues will accept no more gas. The divers are then said to be "saturated."

In this condition, wearing special wetsuits heated by a constant supply of warm water and specifically engineered breathing helmets, equipped with lights, video cameras, and voice communications, divers can enter the sea and work safely for long periods.

Water entry is made through the use of a diving bell. The bell attaches to a transfer tube, which is connected to the habitat. All locks are airtight. Divers leave the living chamber and enter the bell, which is also pressurized to the same level at which the divers will work. The bell is lowered to the job site where the divers slip into the water. When they finish work, they reenter the bell. The bell is lifted to the habitat and the divers return to their living quarters. They cannot be exposed to surface atmospheric pressure, as it would mean certain death. They must live, work, and recreate at the working-level pressure.

Divers generally operate in crews of three and work four- or six-hour shifts. One man stays inside the bell, monitoring pressure, air to the divers, communications, and warm-water flow to the divers' suits. When off duty, they can listen to music through headphones, watch TV through windows in the habitat, eat, sleep, read, etc. Electronic and other devices that might emit a spark and cause a fire in the explosive oxygen-rich atmosphere are not allowed. Immediate evacuation to normal atomospheric pressure would be impossible.

Most habitats, which are like space capsules, are small. A seven-foot-diameter living compartment has bunks on two sides and a separate "wet" compartment for sanitary facilities. And because helium is a light gas, divers' voices become high-pitched. Vocal distortion can be so great communications are jeopardized. So each person is equipped with an electronic voice unscrambler.

At the end of a job, divers remain in their habitat as pressure is slowly decreased over a period of many hours or even days. Once back to normal sea-level pressure, the divers are free to leave the habitat and "surface." Saturation divers are brave individuals who undergo this process several times a year and work in a hostile environment. They are paid accordingly.

20 August 2000—Rescue Site

Before deploying the divers, the rescue group conducted their own TV reconnaissance of the sub. About 0900 hours, a Norwegian specialized undersea TV camera and lighting array was lowered to the wreck. According to a translation of the Russian Navy Museum's summary report on the *Kursk* catastrophe, this effort produced a valuable study of the broken boat. A flaw in the coaming plate of the rear escape hatch was noted. Pictures showed that the entire front end of the submarine, including the first and second compartments, was blown open. An engineer described it as being "like a flower." The petals were hard steel, forced out and backward.

Russian investigators later scrutinized the video images from that survey with a wide range of electronic enhancements. No evidence of a collision between the submarine and another vessel has been announced. It is most probable that had even the slightest sign of such an event been detected, the resulting publicity would have made headlines around the world.

Conversely, if the bow video revealed any hint of a missile strike, that news would likely have been suppressed.

The TV inspection was carried out by the foreign team under Russian supervision. Since the divers were to work on the rear portion of the boat, most of the attention was directed to that area, particularly the escape hatch. This lessened the chance of inadvertent probing for "military secrets."

While the undersea TV pictures were being produced, the commander in chief of the Russian Navy, Admiral Kuroyedov, and Deputy Prime Minister Klebanov, head of the Government *Kursk* Inquiry Commission, were being airlifted to the *Peter the Great*. Klebanov's presence at the site allowed the highest-ranking officers involved to hold a face-to-face, confidential meeting.

In spite of resistance by the Russians, the divers were saturated and on-site. With the TV recon complete, Admiral Skorgen proceeded to execute the dive plan. The first team of three Norwegian divers entered the bell and it was lowered to the *Kursk*. Following standard procedure, two men were set to go into the sea.

A series of checks was carefully performed to ensure all systems were functioning properly. A second inspection made certain the flexible neoprene-canvas body suits were okay. After that, the TV cameras and lights could be activated. Then, trailing an umbilical that contains air hoses, water pipes, lifeline tethers, communications lines, and electric power cables, the men entered the water.

They expected difficulties, so were watchful of the currents that had plagued the Russians. To their relief, they were untroubled. The huge submarine was not lying at some steep angle to the bottom as reported. She rested almost horizontally. And visibility was more than sufficient to work.

The sea floor is a timeless yet ever-changing place. A current may shift and no longer roil the bottom, leaving clear water. This may explain why conditions at the *Kursk* were so different from those described by Russian DSRV personnel. Then again, while not totally impossible, such major changes are rather unlikely.

To learn more about existing circumstances inside the boat, the divers knocked on the outer hull's polymer-coated steel plates with hammers. The sounds indicated the space between the two hulls was filled with water. Conditions inside the inner pressure hull were still unknown.

Approaching the ninth compartment escape hatch, the divers made an examination of the mating ring and the hatch itself. Contrary to earlier Russian reports, both seemed undamaged. The coaming, as seen in the video, had a small fissure.

Working as a team, the two men attempted to open the rescue hatch. It held fast. This gave hope that the escape chute below was not flooded. That might mean the compartment still contained air. Excited, they attempted to vent the hatch, following instructions they had been given by the Russians. The procedure did not work. The information they had been provided was useless.

When their account reached Admiral Skorgen, who was directing diving operations from the *Seaway Eagle*, he was reportedly furious. Divers were risking their lives and the data they were depending on was utterly false. The current wasn't there. Visibility was satisfactory. The escape-hatch mating ring appeared serviceable. The submarine rested at a reasonable angle. And they had been given incorrect hatch venting instructions.

Admiral Skorgen later was reported saying that he telephoned the Northern Fleet Headquarters to state that the rescue mission was in danger unless he was furnished with correct information. His intention was to gain the needed cooperation or end the mission. Further risking of the divers' lives was senseless.

Admiral Popov came aboard the *Seaway Eagle* for a personal meeting with Admiral Skorgen. The two strong military leaders possessed very different temperaments. Popov has been described as volatile, Skorgen as tactful but direct.

There is, however, a great commonality between military officers who are seasoned leaders. They may be from different nations, but their characters have been forged on similar anvils of discipline and duty. That background gives them a unique basis for communicating with each other.

To the Russian, the political implications of this meeting were staggering. What if Skorgen terminated his operation? What if he took his small command back to Norway? The Russian media was already criticizing the Navy and the government for being slow to accept foreign assistance. Now, that aid had arrived on the scene. If the foreigners ended their rescue efforts because their divers were endangered by faulty information provided by the Navy, well . . . An enraged press would crucify any and all involved.

There was also another reality. Russian rescue attempts to enter the *Kursk* had failed. There was no indication further attempts would produce success. Good military leaders are objective and pragmatic. Chances were slim, but there might be crew members alive. If anyone was still living, time was running out. Survivors could not last much longer. On a humanitarian basis, then, logic demanded allowing Skorgen's team to do what they had come to do.

Admiral Popov made a decision that convinced Admiral Skorgen they had matching priorities. Acting quickly, Popov arranged for a helicopter to take two of the group's diving specialists and an interpreter to the Russian sub base at Vidyaevo. There, they were escorted aboard an Oscar II-class submarine, a sister Project 949-A boat to the *Kursk*. They received a hands-on demonstration of the rescue system and were able to study the involved mechanisms. After working all night, they were satisfied. At 0600 hours they returned to the *Seaway Eagle* where they gave a cram course to the divers.

Meantime, a member of the British *LR-5* submersible team was "revolted" to hear the Russians claim they had done everything they could to help the *Kursk*. Arriving with one of the most sophisticated vessels in Europe, which had been designed specifically for rescuing men from sunken submarines, the English team was excluded from the action. "Bitterly disappointed," they had no alternative but to hold station miles from the main activity.

Murmansk Area

The three-star Polyarnye Zori Hotel, located in the center of the city, was some 40 minutes from the Murmansk airport. With seven stories and 199 rooms, it offered a fine view of the Kola fjord. The hotel was a major center for cultural and business activities. It is sited near the Ice Palace, the theater, the art museum, the Museum of Local Lore, and is close to the Navy Museum. For foreigners, a double room, breakfast buffet included, ran about $100 per night. Russian citizens paid approximately half that amount.

On August 20, the majority of the guests were non-Russian. Most of the rooms were taken by foreigners. The same was true at the other three-star lodging, the Arktika, and for the rest of the even halfway decent hotel rooms in the city.

It was not a deluge of tourists, because Murmansk is hardly a tourist haven. In this city of almost a half million, the climate is cold, life is hard, and petty crime was said to be on the rise. The out-of-towners were members of the news media and they had descended on the town like kids flocking to a circus.

Murmansk is the largest Russian seaport on the Arctic Ocean. Ice-free, it can remain open the entire year and is in the center of the Northern Fleet's many bases. The streets reflected the city's strong maritime tradition.

Those same streets also carried a reminder of the number of exhausted nuclear reactors from military ships that have been dumped in the shallow waters, awaiting proper disposal. Radiation counters were located at busily trafficked intersections. And radio stations regularly included radiation levels as part of the weather reports.

Newspaper and electronic media reporters had gathered in Murmansk because that was as close to the rescue site as most could get. Only the Russian state-controlled TV network, RTR, was allowed to broadcast and tape from sea. The nearby home port of the *Kursk*, Vidyaevo, was off-limits to outsiders and guarded by the military.

The disgruntled reporters had little to do except haunt the train station and airport. They questioned travelers, hoping to find relatives of *Kursk* crew members. They also attended the irregularly held press briefings. Since there were few people to interview, they spent most of their time talking with each other. These conversations became incestuous. Someone had a theory about what was really happening. A second person heard it, expanded on it, and it circulated, growing larger and larger until it was replaced by the next new notion.

The press confusion, replete with the government and Navy issuing conflicting stories, had worsened. Disinformation led to a complete distrust of "official" spokespersons.

Many seasoned reporters on this story could remember the days of total Soviet press control. Released from old constraints, they were anxious to cover this breaking event from every angle. They feared that the constant flow of garbled misinformation was a deliberate attempt by officials to keep the issue confused. In other words, it was a cover-up.

The rumor-makers went at it again: the Northern Fleet had shot itself in the foot. They sank the *Kursk* with their own missile. Official denials did nothing to quell the missile theory. In fact, by sticking with the collision-with-foreign-sub position, in the face of no evidence, those who wanted to believe the missile concept were given fresh hope. And they dug deeper to find proof.

A horde of reporters with too little to do tends to ponder every fact. If there was the slightest discrepancy between press releases or comments from officials, it was detected and publicly displayed.

At a news briefing called on August 20 to report on rescue progress, the last vestiges of civility were ripped aside. The press declared open war.

The session was held in a large conference room at the Polyarnye Zori Hotel. An unruly group filled the space to capacity. All present spoke Russian or had personal interpreters. Several of the photographers, in an effort to get an angle over the heads of their fellow journalists, propped chairs along one wall and stood on them. As in every Russian gathering, chain smokers were present, so the air was gray and acrid from smoke. Everyone was talking, so the voice level escalated while they waited, rising in volume, then subsiding, then rising to a louder level.

Management, to protect the hotel's tranquil atmosphere and isolate the commotion, closed the doors to the meeting area. All present understood that starting on time was not even a hope. The briefings began when, and often if, the briefer arrived.

The doors opened, two civilian officials squeezed inside, and the doors closed once more. The speakers, realizing it was impossible to work through the throng of people, elected to stand where they were and issue their statements. There was a rostrum at the other end of the room, but no microphone. So in the chaos, it made little difference.

One of the pair shouted for silence. His request was echoed by the press corps closest to him and the demand eventually reached everyone. A murmuring semisilence followed.

The official read from a single sheet of paper while his assistant passed out copies. There were not nearly enough to go around. Men grabbed the stack and white sheets were flung in the air. A grand melee ensued for possession of one of the pages. This noisy scuffling stopped the reader midsentence. With no voice amplification, half of those in the room couldn't hear him. One reporter yelled to demand more copies of the release. The civil servant shrugged.

Questions were shouted. First one, then a half dozen. They came without waiting for an answer. Flash units began popping and intense lights from video cameras half blinded the two government men, as well as many reporters, who yelled their irritation.

One of the officials waved for silence and the bedlam calmed slightly. He told them that was the release, that was all the available copies, that was all he knew. He and his associate went out the doors and quickly down the corridor to the lobby. A car, with engine running and a third man behind the wheel, waited for them in the hotel drive. They jumped inside just as the mass of journalists erupted, shouting after them, and made their escape.

The reporters knew the routine, too. When they returned, disgruntled, to the lobby, those who grabbed a handout had run off several on a copy machine. The release papers were being peddled for a drink at the bar.

No one knew anything of consequence but they agreed on one point. If they hung around, maybe they'd be in the right spot when something did happen.

They did not have much longer to wait.

21 August 2000—Rescue Site

Shortly after 0700 hours, members of the Norwegian rescue dive team went down to the *Kursk*. Using the correct information, they unsuccessfully attempted a hatch opening. That news was received with great disappointment. It appeared there was no hope of finding survivors.

The divers next decided to use brute force. A crane lowered its cable and hook, which was attached to the closed hatch. Then the crane reeled in the line until it was straining. Slowly the crane increased its power. The steel hatch began to give, then tore loose with a wrenching shriek. The rear upper door was at last open. The escape tube was flooded and empty.

Entering the escape chute, the divers began working on the inner door at the bottom. A second crew was brought in to relieve the first team, and the effort continued. Just over five hours later, they breeched that final barrier. Inside, they found only silt-laden water and poor visibility.

In a somber meeting, Admirals Popov and Skorgen reviewed what was now known. It was agreed that the *Kursk*'s crew had perished and that the Norwegian-British rescue effort was complete. They had fulfilled their mission.

A great wave of sorrow rolled across the water from ship to ship in the flotilla as news of their lost comrades spread. There was little to be done but grieve.

At 2100 hours on August 21, 2001, nine days after the accident, the Russian Military Council of the Northern Fleet issued a statement. It officially recognized the loss of the crew. Condolences were extended to all relatives.

Television is the universal Russian news medium. It reaches into the most remote parts of the nation and exerts a strong influence on public opinion. Television reporter Arkady Mamontov with RTR network had been giving reports during the operation from the deck of *Peter the Great*. A respected and well-watched personality, he delivered the terrible news. There was no hope of survivors.

The dark days of August had come to Russia once again.

CHAPTER 9

21–22 August 2000—Rescue Site

THE MOOD AT THE RESCUE SITE WAS AS GLOOMY AS THE weather. The news that President Vladimir Putin had declared Wednesday, August 23, a national day of mourning for the lost crew members of the *Kursk* did little to raise the men's spirits.

Norwegian and British workers took the failure of their mission personally. Many sat in morose silence. They pondered what might have been done and how they could have contributed to a speedier operation.

In the midst of this grief the divers were called upon for one final act. A team made a last descent to the *Kursk*. There, they closed the hatch and welded it shut to prevent scavengers, a term that included U.S. as well as NATO intelligence agencies, from entering the boat.

That night, after the end of rescue activity, Russian Minister of Defense Igor Sergeyev appeared on TV. According to reports, he made several stunning declarations.

The first was that debris had been located on the sea floor. Lying less than 300 feet from the *Kursk*'s bow was what was presumed to be a piece of the conning tower or "sail" of a foreign submarine. Some sources described what had supposedly been discovered as part of a conning tower railing. That was new. The next two items were not. Apparently harking back to dispatches from the two search aircraft that located the general area of the *Kursk* disaster, he noted the discovery of a lurking sub as well as the white and green marker buoy. This is the same buoy, mentioned earlier, that was later identified as a sack of potatoes that had fallen overboard while provisions were being loaded onto the *Peter the Great*.

Either the Defense minister was provided with false information or he had acquiesced to the collision theory and was lending his support, or both. In any case, his statement added credence to the unsubstantiated claims.

At dawn on August 22, ten days after the accident, a formal on-site memorial ceremony was held for the lost submariners. When it was completed, the *Normand Pioneer*, with the British *LR-5* secured aboard, and the *Seaway Eagle* completed preparations for their return to Norway. After again expressing their condolences, they departed the tragic site at 1400 hours. Other ships of the Northern Fleet were leaving as well.

A rear guard, consisting of the hydrographic survey vessel *Mars* and a rotating escort of at least one and at times two warships, was to remain. The location had been pinpointed by satellite mapping. A buoy marked the precise place where the hulk rested on the sea floor. The *Mars* was to monitor radiation in the area. To this point, no contamination had been detected.

The warships on sentinel duty were there for a different purpose. The Russians were all too aware of the top-secret American CIA operation in 1974 that had recovered a sunken Soviet submarine for intelligence purposes. This fantastic maritime feat had stunned the Soviet high command. That boat had been retrieved from a depth of over 17,000 feet. The *Kursk* lay at 300 feet. Here was a much more tempting prize, as it was the latest ship of the line.

A recovery would not be necessary. It was feared that divers might be sent to inspect the *Kursk*. Deeply submerged underwater, they could avoid sonar detection. What might they find in the wreckage? Obviously more than the Russians wanted to reveal.

So the site was left with a full-time guard. And to make doubly certain, the ship on duty dropped hand grenades and depth charges into the water at unpredictable intervals. The resulting explosions would kill or injure aquatic spies.

As the last of the flotilla departed, one vessel sounded a mournful horn and siren. It was unheard in the eternal silence of the depths.

Russian Federation

The announcement by the Military Council of the Northern Fleet that the entire crew had perished sorrowed the Russian people.

The *Kursk* disaster had come at a time when those in the news media were desperately struggling to establish the limits of how far they could go in reporting a story. In a sense, coverage of the *Kursk* catastrophe was a window of opportunity. This single event established a relatively sharp line of demarcation between pro-government and opposing-government media.

A news service's favorable view of military actions during the rescue effort was one litmus test. Another measure was backing the collision theory. These two criteria marked the news outlets supportive of the government.

Critiques of the official point of view or critical stories about Navy bungling pointed out the media less inclined toward the government. Readers, listeners, and viewers received a practical demonstration of where each news service was positioned.

The enormous amount of coverage of the *Kursk* disaster also induced a powerful change in Russian attitude. What started as sadness was transformed into indignation and outrage. The targets of this emotional frustration were the military and the government.

There is an old public relations adage about not arguing with the person who holds the microphone. In this case, both pro-government and anti-government media had microphones and TV cameras, which allowed them to openly argue with each other. Then, to everyone's amazement, the print media, usually bitterly divided, became unified. Their questions reflected the nation's wrath and confusion. Why didn't the Navy have the equipment required for the rescue? Why wasn't foreign assistance immediately accepted? Why did the president blithely continue his vacation?

Izvestia, normally a government ally, featured a photo of President Putin in a Navy hat and barked, "False information about the tragedy of the *Kursk* is sinking the military's reputation."

Moskovsky Komsomolets featured three pictures: one of Defense Minister Sergeyev at a billiards table, another of Admiral Kuroyedov, and a third of President Putin on vacation in Sochi. The caption was caustic: "They don't sink."

The absolute barrage of personal criticism did not please President Putin. In striking back against his more adamant critics, he accused the media of political blackmail.

There are three dominant TV networks in Russia. RTR is state controlled. ORT is "public television," although it is 51 percent owned by the state. NTV was at that time the independent commercial channel and the subject of government scrutiny. Air talent from NTV complained of being excluded from news scenes and the village of Vidyaevo during the rescue operation.

Ignoring the negative press, a segment of the military establishment continued its efforts to place blame for the disaster on foreigners. Head of the Northern Fleet, Admiral Popov, added a new high to the collision story by stating he would, if need be, spend the rest of his days on earth trying to find who "organized" the sinking of the *Kursk*.

This was later countered in the news media by publishing the Norwegian Navy's dismissal of the collision story as "propaganda" for Russians.

Government-controlled RTR furnished the only TV coverage from the rescue flotilla that was allowed. An RTR team broadcast live from the *Peter the Great*. In the aftermath of the failed mission, RTR presented a chronology of the operation's events to the Russian public. It amounted to a slight reordering of recent history by fudging dates to make it appear there was less confusion and more immediate action by the Navy.

This new sequence of events produced a quick back-lash. *Time Europe* responded by stating, "The strangest and most cynical-seeming piece of damage control so far appeared on the state-owned TV network, RTR, early this week." The same source also implied the aim of the chronology was to present the notion that a prompt rescue operation took place.

Time Europe also noted that RTR had indicated the Russian Navy accepted offers of foreign aid on Tuesday, August 15, three days after the accident—this in the face of Deputy Prime Minister Klebanov's assurance to the public on Wednesday, August 16, that no such assistance was necessary and the Navy possessed all needed ships and matériel. This thrust and counterthrust blitz from officials and news services created a perfect climate for the generation of progressively complex theories.

One account held that the accident put the entire naval command into a state of shock. The loss of the *Kursk*, the recurrent downed-by-a-friendly-missile story, a rumor that Admiral Popov had tried to shoot himself in despair, the misreporting of undersea conditions to cover an inability to dock with the sub, and more, all combined to indicate the Navy was at fault.

Possibilities such as these had a depressing impact on the society as a whole and a devastating effect on one group in particular. Families of the lost crew needed nothing to add to their grief.

Relatives of *Kursk* crew members had begun arriving in Murmansk by train before the official announcement that all hope was lost. They came to comfort the wives and children of the fallen submariners and to be close to the source of further news.

At first, the Navy was unprepared to assist family members who arrived at the train station. Disconsolate men and women were left to fend for themselves. Some bereaved relatives had to contend with taxi drivers demanding the princely sum of 500 rubles for the drive to Vidyaevo. Five hundred rubles was the equivalent of $18, about a fifth of an officer's monthly pay, an outrageous price for the trip.

By Saturday, August 19, the Navy's oversight was rectified. Special direction signs to buses had been posted in the railroad terminal and personnel were on hand to aid these pilgrims.

After serious deliberation, it was decided that President Putin would fly to Northern Fleet Naval Headquarters at Severomorsk. Dressed in a black suit and shirt with no tie, he was greeted by Admiral Kuroyedov, head of the Russian Navy, then transported to Vidyaevo. Putin intended to meet with the families on Tuesday, August 22, before the scheduled national day of mourning. In preparation for this session, relatives of the deceased not yet in the Murmansk area, or in transit, would be offered air transportation. Money was short, so Karat Airlines Flight AKT 9611 was chartered by an oil company. A naval officer from headquarters later noted that the Navy did not have an aircraft large enough to accommodate the number of people.

Families traveled to Moscow from all regions of Russia and, despite their mourning, told each other their stories. Many were too exhausted from watching TV reports of the rescue as it slowly progressed. One woman complained that no one had contacted her about the flight. She found out about it from television. A tearful man stated he had learned from the paper that his nephew was among the missing.

In an effort to help the grieving throng, civilian and military psychologists were assigned to the group.

The news media, still hungry for coverage, came out in force. Many waited to waylay family members at Vnukovo Airport in Moscow, where the chartered flight originated. This was an opportunity for reporters in the capital city to file firsthand stories on the aftermath of the disaster. With no one to hold them back, they worked the crowd, seeking human interest tales and more evidence of military disregard for surviving family members.

Once in Murmansk, however, preparations improved. There were no available hotel rooms. Media representatives had most of those. So many family members were lodged with local citizens.

On the morning of August 22, all was set for the meeting with President Putin. For security reasons, the session was held in the closed town of Vidyaevo.

Just one TV network, government-run RTR, was present, with a single camera. To handle the feedback to the broadcast center in Moscow, since there was no satellite transmitter available in the tightly controlled town, RTR used a remote truck from RTL, a German telecaster. This allowed the RTL Moscow bureau chief to view actual real-time coverage of the closed session. He was quoted as saying, "The only camera that was there belonged to RTR. At the same time, the head of the state broadcasting company, Oleg Dobrodeyev, was personally sitting in the

RTL transmission van, controlling every frame that was sent to Moscow."

TV coverage was said to have depicted a sympathetic president consoling the bereaved relatives and family in a calm atmosphere.

Only a few reporters were present for the meeting. No tape recorders were allowed. However, according to several reports in *The Moscow Times*, one journalist secretly taped the session. And what purports to be a transcript of the exchange appeared in the Russian press. In the account it is clear that President Putin had not anticipated the degree of anger and resentment confronting him.

The session opened badly. Putin noted that he had a meeting at Fleet Headquarters and thought he should see the family group first.

Questions were shouted, objections yelled, Putin was interrupted, and people hollered at each other. The meeting appeared to have ended leaving many unsatisfied and a bit shocked.

In summary, the president proposed a financial settlement to the families based on 120 months' pay of an average military officer. This caused an immediate and lengthy debate over what an average officer earned. Putin also agreed to make at least one of the Dagdizel specialists who had been on the *Kursk* part of the crew so that individual's family would qualify for compensation.

Each family was awarded an additional 725,000 rubles (a little more than $26,000) along with housing anywhere in the country. Many charitable funds were also being set up to help relatives of *Kursk* victims.

Inadvertently, this effort to mollify the relatives of those lost men was to have a far-reaching effect. News of money being paid to ease the lives of the *Kursk* relations caused a backlash from mothers whose sons had died fighting in Chechnya.

Relatives of soldiers and sailors killed in the line of duty didn't question that *Kursk* crew members' families deserved reparation. Compensation was expected as part of the system. Family units losing a member receive the standard 120 times the deceased's monthly salary, to be divided among immediate family. Each family member also received an insurance settlement of 25 times the serviceman's monthly pay. And a lump sum amount was allowed for funeral expenses.

The upgrading of benefits to families of those who died on the *Kursk* to officer level for the purposes of fixing compensation, along with the $26,000, and guarantee of housing, seemed inequitable to many.

Their discrimination cause was quickly taken up by Pravo Materi, the Foundation for a Mother's Right, a volunteer organization formed in 1989 to provide legal aid to families of soldiers killed in uniform.

During the meeting, Putin also spoke harshly several times about the media, accusing them of falsehoods and taking advantage of the disaster for political gain. After reading the meeting transcript, some commentators felt he did not take criticism very well. Nor did the president have a satisfactory answer to the question of how and where qualified relatives should apply for the settlement. And one interesting press criticism concerned Putin's use of vulgar language.

According to a translation of the transcript, Putin stayed with the Navy line. During a confused exchange, he placed blame for the disaster on a collision or perhaps a mine or possibly an onboard explosion, which he noted specialists thought very unlikely although theoretically possible.

Several of the relatives clearly did not want to believe the entire crew was dead. There were calls to cancel the National Day of Mourning. However, as Putin pointed out, it was already Wednesday, August 23, the scheduled day, in some parts of Russia. He suggested instead that he forward the families' request that TV coverage not expand by playing requiems.

Perhaps the most chilling and unnerving incident of the entire turbulent day took place during a later press conference. A woman identified as Nadezhda Tylik, mother of Senior Lieutenant Sergey N. Tylik, who was the electric navigation party commander on board the *Kursk*, attended a post-meeting press conference. She began shouting at Deputy Prime Minister Ilya Klebanov. The television camera caught the action. A naval officer slipped to her side. A woman, armed with a long-needled hypodermic syringe, moved behind Mrs. Tylik and injected her with what was reportedly a sedative. As Mrs. Tylik said later, the shot made her instantly unable to speak. She dropped to the floor and was carried out. A Navy official told several journalists that it was not as big a deal as the West made it. "We are simply protecting the relatives from undue pain—it was for her own protection."

To counter the bad publicity, her husband, Nikolai, a 20-year submarine veteran who spoke after the meeting, maintained he had requested that his wife be sedated because he feared for her health. Months later, according to several news services, Mrs. Tylik said Nikolai later told her he had lied to save her from getting further upset. He had not asked that she be sedated.

While the meeting and that entire day had been somewhat messy, subsequent opinion polls in Russia indicated it did little to harm Putin's popularity. Findings reported by the All-Russia Center for Public Opinion Research (VtsIOM) showed their sample lowered approval of his overall job performance from a peak of 73 in July to 65. Considering the length and depth of media attacks on his performance during the *Kursk* disaster, the loss was surprisingly small.

While President Putin was dealing with the families, who were demanding to know why he had not personally taken charge of the recovery effort, another unusual event was developing.

Later that same day, August 22, Minister of Defense Igor Sergeyev, along with Admirals Kuroyedov and Popov, submitted their resignations. The following day, President Putin spoke on RTR TV. He noted the resignations and made it clear he had refused to accept them. He said he did not intend to fire anyone without having a clear establishment of guilt. Many responded to that position with knowing looks. They understood about Russian resignations.

Putin was quoted as saying that rather than blaming these officials, anger should be directed at those who had destroyed the Army, Navy, and the state. By this, he clearly meant the group labeled oligarchs. The "oligarchy" is a class of superwealthy businessmen, created after the fall of the Soviet Union during the process of modernization and democratization. Some of these powerful men gained their wealth through political connections and shrewd business deals, putting together vast commercial empires by acquisition of cheap state assets. Oligarchs were blamed by the Kremlin for corruption of the media, the legislature, and the judicial branch, along with skimming profits from state resources, stealing by tax avoidance, and much more.

The national day of mourning was painful, as a country publicly showed its grief. Keeping with tradition, mourners flocked to Russian Orthodox churches. Candles were lit and thousands upon thousands said prayers for the dead and their loved ones. The event was so sobering the press paused in its pointed criticism of how badly the entire disaster had been handled.

23–31 August 2000—Moscow

On Wednesday evening, August 23, during the appearance on RTR TV in which he rejected the resignations of Sergeyev, Kuroyedov, and Popov, President Putin was somber. He revealed that he felt a personal responsibility for the loss of the *Kursk* and her crew. He assured the Russian people that those at fault would be identified and punished. When questioned about the meeting in Vidyaevo with the families, he responded by saying words were not enough; they were difficult to find. He wanted to wail.

Devoted to his goal of improving morale in his country, he blamed the negative press on two media magnates who wanted political gain. He also noted that Russia had survived a lot and would overcome this loss to be great once again.

While not mentioned during the TV interview but

hinted at in other ways, plans were being laid. There was one act that would hopefully stem the aggressive media pressure on the government and the military. The deep desire expressed over and over during the meeting with the families was to have the bodies of their loved ones retrieved.

To accomplish this recovery, and satisfy the living, would be no small task. Conditions inside the *Kursk* were dangerous for divers. Debris was strewn throughout the boat and the workers would have to be careful not to snag their diving suits or long umbilical hoses as they moved about. Entry into some of the spaces and compartments would require cutting holes through the double hulls. The project would be expensive, risk lives, and take time. It would also require weeks to set up. It had to be done, though. From the standpoint of media relations and the grieving families, the sooner the better.

Twelve days after the accident, on August 24, a Thursday morning, a formal memorial service attended by the relatives took place in Vidyaevo. Groundbreaking for a monument to the *Kursk* and its lost crew was part of the ceremony.

Relatives who wished could also participate in shipboard rites at the disaster site. Wreaths were lowered into the sea. Sad, gray-faced widows, children, mothers, and fathers stood in a tight group against the chill wind. Their tearful eyes were focused on the water, as if each were trying to peer into the depths for a last view of their loved ones.

A Russian Orthodox priest and a Moslem cleric gave prayers for the deceased. Then the ship made a slow circle around the spot now marked with floral tributes and sounded its horn before returning to port.

Concurrent with the various memorial tributes and with little public fanfare, military prosecutors opened a criminal investigation into the tragedy. A short while later, one of the panel's lines of inquiry was fed to the news media. The committee was looking into charges that human error had been the decisive cause of the sinking. The accident could have been due to a "violation of safety rules."

This leak, preplanned or not, was the first inkling that the collision theory might not have gained a united front throughout the Russian military organization.

The memorial services appeared to mark a slowdown in the news value of the *Kursk* disaster. During the next few days there were only stories of minor interest or concern on the accident. The government Emergency Situations Minister Sergey Shoigu indicated that a program was moving forward to establish several sea-rescue centers to handle any future accidents.

Of specific importance to the *Kursk*, reports began to surface about sabotage on the submarine by pro-Chechen militant rebels from Dagestan. Russian troops had been fighting to quell a revolutionary movement in Chechnya. A terrorist group claimed the submarine was sunk by one of the crew who came from Dagestan. Since only one crew member and the two torpedo experts from Dagdizel had Dagestan connections, this was a rather pointed accusation.

Actually, sabotage stories had been surfacing before this release. The earliest had been from the Ukraine and appeared immediately after the early news about the submarine being down. That story also assigned the reason for the disaster to a terrorist group.

The sabotage concept reinforced what was already fact. An explosion occurred on board the *Kursk*. Sabotage, as a cause of that explosion, was in several ways better than the collision theory. Here too, blame for the catastrophe was attributed to a foreign source. If that foreign source was hostile to Russia, so much the better. That theory would reiterate to the Russian people that enemies of their nation are ruthless—and that Russia needs military strength for self-protection. Therefore, funding the military should and must take top priority.

In order to follow all leads, or to give the seemingly groundless sabotage rumors a degree of official credence, the Russian FSB, their Federal Security Service, was called in to investigate. Dagdizel, which had almost slipped from sight concerning the *Kursk*, was now back in the center ring. The acting director of Dagdizel, Rustam Usmanov, was quoted in *The Moscow Times* defending the Dagdizel experts on board: "These two people were patriots on a sacred mission. Only scum could say that they were kamikaze bombers, and the scum must be drowned in junk." Another spokesperson called the investigation unwarranted and provided the names of the two experts who had perished, calling them "saints!"

27 August 2000

First morning light came early to Moscow. The skyline of the city is a mix of old and new buildings. One of the newest, its towering spire topped by a TV mast, rose high above all others. It was a minaret redefined by modern ar-

chitecture. For the last three decades, the Ostankino
Tower had been a Moscow landmark. At a little over
1,700 feet from the tip of the antenna to the ground, it
was the second tallest broadcast mast in the world. The
Seventh Heaven restaurant and an adjacent observation
deck had made this a tourist destination. Housing transmission systems for TV and radio signals to some 18 million people in the Moscow area, the structure was also a
key element in providing service for 16 of Moscow's 25
paging companies.

During the early afternoon, at 1520 hours Moscow
time, a fire, thought to have been caused by a short cir-
cuit, broke out. The blaze started in a narrow part of the
tower, some 300 feet above the restaurant. Muscovites
could see dense smoke issuing from the concrete structure from all over the city. The built-in fire extinguishing
system either malfunctioned or ran out of foam, allowing
the blaze time to intensify.

Most tower visitors were safely evacuated. A few people, identified as firefighters and an elevator operator,
were trapped inside an elevator car. Before they could be
rescued, the car dropped almost a thousand feet, crashing
in the basement several yards below street level. This,
along with the fall of two more elevators, started a separate fire on the ground. The exact number inside the elevator was difficult to establish. The 300-ton elevator
counterweight, traveling at a speed far exceeding 100
miles per hour, followed the car down the shaft and
landed on top. When the doors were pried open, only
fragments of bodies were found. Later forensic work revealed three had perished.

In the end, 415 firemen worked nonstop and finally

tapped out the fire after a grueling 26 hours of exhausting work. All their equipment had to be carried up endless steps as firefighters risked their lives working so high above the ground.

Damage to the tower was staggering. Several experts questioned if the structure could ever be repaired. Others hoped it could be restored. But no one doubted the upset caused by this new disaster. Moscow suffered a massive broadcast radio and TV blackout. Only citizens with satellite dishes were able to receive programming. Paging was severely interrupted, affecting some police and emergency service units.

Since the average Russian spends five hours a day viewing TV, loss of the medium had a huge social impact on the people of Moscow. Having the state-controlled channels off the air was intolerable to the politicians. Putin called for restoration of all services within a week. An emergency transmitter was attached to the building and three days later, RTR and ORT public television were back on the air, sharing a single channel.

NTV, the privately owned TV provider, utilized its satellite signal delivery capability, and since the service had not been given antenna space on the now-burned tower, NTV also had a small transmitter in Moscow. The independent facility stayed on the air. Viewers with dishes, and many Moscow homes, could receive NTV programming, much to the chagrin of government leaders. Demand for satellite receivers quickly began to exceed supplies.

From the government's standpoint, there was one benefit from this added trouble. The fire took the focus off the *Kursk* catastrophe. Jokes about the fire, however, were pointed. Poking at the collision theory, one held that Washington had officially "confirmed that no American TV tower ever came close to Ostankino!"

When TV service was restored, though, the *Kursk* saga regained momentum.

Each of the *Kursk* crewmen was posthumously awarded the Order of Courage medal. Captain Lyachin was given the Order of Hero of Russia. This, along with the monument being built by presidential decree, was seen by some as an effort to twist the *Kursk* catastrophe into a heroic event in which the men died defending their country. In a real sense, this was true. The men of the *Kursk* were brave. And they were on their country's duty. The resistance came from a military overtone that hinted they were at war.

The next event gave officials concerned with avoiding the placement of blame for the sinking another sabotage possibility. A Web site, operated by Chechen rebels, announced that their well-known field operations commander, Shamil Basayev, was behind the Ostankino blaze. According to the site, his command issued a statement that the rebels had paid a sum equal to $25,000 to an employee who worked in the tower. This individual supposedly carried out the act of terrorism that started the fire.

The rebels' Web site also again credited its militants with causing the *Kursk* disaster, repeating the story that a sailor from Dagestan had volunteered to destroy the sub.

Even though the government responded with immediate denials, questions were once again being asked about the *Kursk*. What had the Government Inquiry Commission learned? When would a full report be made public? If the Chechen rebels were not to blame, who was?

The situation smoldered for a few days. Then came September—and a news report from *Berliner Zeitung*, a respected German newspaper.

1–15 September 2000

According to the German publication, the Russian Federal Security Service (FSB) issued a confidential report to President Putin. This classified document was said to have been developed under the supervision of FSB Chief Nikolai Patrushev. The contents, if true, were devastating.

By the *Berliner Zeitung* account, the report indicated that during fleet maneuvers on Saturday, August 12, a cruise missile, fired from the flagship, *Peter the Great*, accidently homed on the *Kursk*. A new model Granit-type missile traveled some 12.5 miles and either an error in the warhead or failure of the friend-or-foe identifier aboard the *Kursk* caused the hit.

The newspaper reported that a small blast occurred after the missile entered the water. That was followed by an immensely more powerful undersea explosion. Both detonations were observed from the bridge on the *Peter the Great*, which had been test firing missiles since August 2.

There is an implication to this story that requires clarification. A person standing on the beach at ocean's edge can look out at the horizon and spot objects about six miles away. The curvature of the earth limits line of sight to approximately that distance. Even a powerful telescope won't help someone see farther. The only way to overcome the Earth's curve is to gain a higher vantage point. Climbing onto a lifeguard platform 12 feet above the sandy beach provides additional miles in distant viewing.

The bridge of the *Peter the Great* cruiser is more than 50 feet above the waves. A lookout stationed there with binoculars could easily see a missile hit the sea 12 miles away. An observer would have no trouble recognizing the geyser of foaming white water that would be thrown upward by an explosion as large as the one that tore open the *Kursk*. Only those sufficiently high above the main deck, though, would have a sight line enabling them to view a distant strike.

As noted earlier, an officer on the *Peter the Great* claimed to be an eyewitness to a missile fall and a great undersea blast. It is possible this account was included in the alleged FSB report. And since the *Peter the Great* was the first ship to reach the *Kursk* site, there was talk that members of the ship's command knew where to search.

The newspaper story was quickly denied by Deputy Prime Minister Klebanov, as head of the Government Inquiry Commission, and Defense Minister Igor Sergeyev. According to Klebanov, his group was centering on three possible causes: collision with another vessel, hitting an old World War II mine, or just possibly an inadvertent explosion on board the *Kursk*. Klebanov promised to have a more specific answer as soon as his committee completed its study.

Despite official denials, other news stories, concerning torpedoes fired from the *Peter the Great* striking the *Kursk*, began to appear.

Another glimpse into the workings of the propaganda machinery was granted during this time period. Several

Russian newspapers published an unsubstantiated "secret" story about American President Bill Clinton. During an alleged telephone conversation with President Putin, Clinton supposedly admitted that a U.S. sub had collided with the *Kursk*, sinking the Russian submarine. To make amends for this accident, Clinton intervened in the Star Wars missile defense program and brought it to a complete stop.

This was an excellent example of sophisticated damage control. The purported deal between Putin and Clinton was secret. Anyone who believed that story would therefore understand why no physical proof of a collision would ever surface. It was not because there was no evidence. It was because the Russian government was concealing what they had found as part of their confidential agreement with the U.S.

It would be difficult to find a better illustration of how far officials backing the collision theory were willing to go to establish their position as fact. Not all the military, however, had bought off on the matter.

On Sunday, September 3, an interview with Admiral Vladimir Yegorov, commander of the Russian Baltic Fleet, was aired on RTR television. In one stunning statement, he declared that the *Kursk* could have been hit by a missile fired from another Russian ship. Acknowledging such a strike was unlikely during Russian Navy exercises in the Barents Sea, he strongly indicated that such an event could not be ruled out.

Why the Baltic Fleet commander might have even suggested such a possibility is a mystery. The mere hint that a friendly missile could have been involved was against all official pronouncements.

One reason for such a severe break with ranks might be money. In a military strapped for cash, there must be competition for funds at every level. Damaging the Northern Fleet's reputation might somehow assist the Baltic Fleet's quest for capital.

Whatever the motivation, having an admiral mention a missile as a possible cause for the disaster did not go unnoticed. In response, efforts to reinforce the collision theory were now more vigorous than ever.

On September 4, unnamed Defense Ministry officials used the *Itar-Tass* news service to remake an astonishing claim. A story stated parts of a metal railing that could have broken off the top of a foreign sub during a collision had been recovered from the *Kursk* site. Admittedly, a hunk of railing is not as spectacular as finding fragments of a conning tower as previously claimed by Defense Minister Igor Sergeyev days before. But since no public evidence of the conning tower wreckage had been produced and no further mention was made of that discovery, a rail was better than nothing.

In an effort to cooperate with the Russians to the fullest possible extent, President Clinton's National Security Adviser Sandy Berger met with Security Council Secretary Sergei Ivanov in New York on September 6. In their session, Berger provided the Russian with information about the *Kursk* sinking that was collected by U.S. intelligence-gathering ships. A U.S. naval officer supplied his Russian counterpart with detailed information compiled from the wide range of acoustical data recorded at the time.

This conciliatory move was apparently insufficient. Nine days later, two members of the Russian Duma, the lower chamber of the legislature, demanded that the United States allow a close inspection of the submarine *Memphis*. This despite the earlier photo session in Norway that showed no damage.

The United States, naturally, refused. Recognizing the ever-ready presence of spies, it was not desirable to have Russian "experts," supposedly seeking collision-damage evidence, exploring one of America's more sophisticated submarines.

While the propaganda wonder workers were busy chopping at each other with words and rumors, important work of another kind was being plotted. All other Oscar-II-class boats had been placed on suspended duty and called back to their home ports.

Ranking naval officers harbored a degree of fear about what had happened on the lost submarine. Was the explosion an isolated incident? Was there some inherent defect in the torpedoes or their handling and storage programs? Had the catastrophe been caused by sabotage? Did that mean they had to watch their crews more closely?

The magnitude of the *Kursk* disaster had dampened the morale of many submariners. There was less enthusiasm for extended undersea duty. And adding to the personnel side of the problem, leaving submarines that cost billions of rubles bobbing at dockside was a total waste of defense capabilities.

The Russian Navy had a serious need to know what really happened. Gesturing and posturing could continue in public, but privately, answers were needed. And those answers were needed quickly.

CHAPTER 10

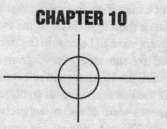

16 September 2000–5 October 2000

IN AN ALL-OUT EFFORT TO RESOLVE ITS PROBLEMS, THE Russian Navy was about to launch a major, classified, clandestine activity. The fact that there was no way to hide part of the venture made this extremely difficult. Worse, the function they had to perform in the open was going to attract the scrutiny of the world press.

Ideally, the total undertaking would have been done in secret. The resources to bring it off, however, were simply not available. Accomplishing the mission required a high level of technical expertise, expensive, dangerous-to-use cutting tools, and a specialized ship. A compromise plan was needed, one that would provide an airtight cover story. It was decided to use the stage magician's old standby, misdirection.

A salvage operation, to recover the bodies of the *Kursk* crewmen, would hold the attention of the news media.

While focus was on that project, the secret activity would be done out of sight, under 350 feet of water.

The Navy wanted Russian divers inside the sunken *Kursk*. Publicly, they would be there searching for bodies. That was a popular goal. Privately, those divers would conduct a classified four-part mission.

Part one was a thorough check of the twin nuclear reactors. The divers were to be certain the two units had not been damaged by the emergency scram shutdown. If problems existed, the Russians did not want the world to know. Even if the reactors were all right, it would not do to have the media learn Russian technicians were even looking at them. The resulting stories would cast serious doubt on their repeated assurances of safety. So either way, the inspection needed to be accomplished without attracting notice.

Part two was the recovery of any remaining encoding devices or books, manuals for operating the boat's systems or weaponry, and the ship's log. If these documents had not been destroyed in the blast, they had to be located and retrieved. Past experience had shown that the United States would spend unimaginable sums of money to acquire such information from a sunken hulk. Who could tell what the U.S. might try this time. Drilling a hole through the center of the earth to gain entry via the underside of the submarine was apparently not beyond them.

Even though the codes had been instantly and automatically changed during the first hours of the *Kursk* disaster, old codes still had value. NATO and the Americans had thousands of hours of taped transmissions just waiting to be deciphered. Newly interpreted information would give valuable insights into Russian plans and preparedness.

Part three centered on a hunt for any evidence, no matter how slight, to support the collision theory. Performing such a search openly would be tantamount to an admission of lacking adequate proof to support the accusation. And, if such evidence was discovered, it was better to keep it confidential until the most advantageous moment for revelation.

Finally, the Navy desperately needed to define the cause of the explosions which they knew had occurred. Determining a reason for the blasts would allow modifications to programs and hardware that would help prevent future disasters. Understanding the cause would restore morale among the submariners and allow the *Kursk*'s sister submarines a quicker return to sea duty.

The brief entry into Compartment 9 through the escape hatch had demonstrated an absolute need for additional access to the interior. Moving about had been difficult because of the debris. Going from one compartment to another, due to the closed watertight doors, was impossible.

Diver safety was also an issue. Every yard a diver stepped away from his entry point meant that another three feet of umbilical, containing the air hose, water line, and power-video-communications cables, had to be played out. If any of these vital connections happened to snag or were damaged, the diver would be effectively out of action. If the air or warm water supply were interrupted, the diver would die.

The ideal method for gaining access would allow a diver to enter the inside pressure hull through several portals. The closer an opening to the search site, the less the length of his umbilical and therefore a lessened risk of accidents.

To conduct this extensive operation, the Navy called upon Rubin Central Design Bureau for assistance. Originally responsible for laying out plans for the *Kursk* and her sister boats, the Rubin Bureau was the logical choice. A team of engineers and marine architects was now given what was for them a sort of reverse challenge. Their usual assignment was to create submarines. Here they were being asked, in a sense, to dismantle one.

Rubin managers immediately began planning how best to cut through the sub's outer hull, then slice into the inner hull to gain access. Top Central Design Bureau personnel started a critical review of the submarine's original engineering drawings with three ideas in mind.

They needed to locate places to make the outer hull incisions in areas free of bracing and other structural impediments so cutting would be less difficult. Ideally, they would breach the outer hull in places where a diver might move between the two hulls for some distance along the length of the boat. Free access would allow them to make several holes in the inner hull from one opening in the outer shell. Finally, for simplicity, they wanted to find the best locations for piercing the inner hull so as to avoid bulkheads and support members. The goal was to make full-size templates that could then be placed against the side of the submarine to assist in locating the exact cutting sites.

The Rubin team's next task was to deal with the divers. Not just any divers would do.

Each of the mission goals required the skills of trained

experts: one in the field of nuclear reactor design, one with an advanced understanding of damage evaluation and marine architecture, and a third with knowledge of explosives allied with arson investigation. Finding divers with this expertise proved to be impossible.

Since it would take too long to train the needed experts in saturation diving, the decision was made to teach several divers the basics of reactor design, marine architecture, and the rest of the needed specialities. The divers would enter the wreck and conduct their inspections. Video images and verbal comments would be relayed to the real experts who would be on-site in the mother ship. These specialists could then request more information or different views to arrive at their conclusions. Although complicated, this plan was the best available option.

Divers for the mission were selected from members of the 328th Emergency Search and Rescue detachment of the Russian Navy and immediately began their necessary crash courses.

Since part of the mission was body retrieval, those who would enter the *Kursk* needed basic forensic skills. To help each man overcome the emotional and psychological burden of handling dead bodies, volunteers from the diving detachment were assigned to work in a morgue and take classes at St. Petersburg Scientific Institute No. 40.

Because parts of the operation were clouded by secrecy, a dive plan was developed that allowed only Russians inside the submarine. As each hole was completed, one Russian diver would enter the hulk, equipped with lights, video, and a 60-plus-foot umbilical to allow for freedom of motion. A second Russian would remain at the opening, tending the umbilical, ready to render assistance. All non-Russian divers would stay outside.

Inside the submarine, body parts would be collected and hauled to the surface in plastic bags. Bodies would be placed in special containers to help preserve forensic information. After a hole had been used, it would be sealed to prevent others from reentering.

The danger inherent in roaming inside the destroyed sub was evident. As recently as 1986, two Russian divers were killed during an excursion into a surface ship that had sunk in the Black Sea. Every precaution was needed to prevent deadly mishaps.

While this operation was under way, Rubin was also acting as government adviser on negotiations with Stolt Offshore of Norway. Since Stolt had furnished divers and equipment for the original entry into the *Kursk*, the company was the first choice for the body recovery assignment. Russian divers were scheduled to depart for the Stolt training base on Saturday, September 16. It was a surprise to many when, with little warning, the divers were told not to go. Their mission was canceled.

The Norwegian Division of Stolt Offshore was reportedly asking the equivalent of $12 million to perform the recovery work. Rubin estimated the job should cost about $9 million. This price differential may well have been caused by Stolt's previous experience with Russia's lack of cooperation during the rescue effort. The two groups failed to reach an agreement on price and negotiations were stalled.

Wednesday, September 20, marked the fortieth day after the *Kursk* sinking on August 12.

A tenet of the Russian Orthodox faith is that the soul

of a departed person leaves the body and ascends to heaven on the fortieth day after death. So on this date, from one end of the nation to the other, mourning services were held. People filled country roadside chapels and huge city cathedrals.

On the military base at Vidyaevo, priests chanted liturgies in ceremonies attended by families of lost loved ones. The city of *Kursk* held packed services fortified by the special bond between the town and the submarine.

In a touching moment, a large granite slab, set in the sand dunes outside the town of Severodvinsk, where the *Kursk* was first laid down in 1992, was unveiled as a monument to the missing men. It is inscribed, "This sorrowful stone is set in memory of the crew of the nuclear submarine *Kursk*, who tragically died on August 12, 2000, while on military duty."

During the day, in contrast to the churchgoers, crowds of protesters gathered outside the U.S. Embassy in Moscow, demanding an inquiry into whether or not a U.S. submarine had rammed the *Kursk*.

The mission to recover bodies was scheduled to begin in less than two weeks. But controversy over risking the divers' lives, as opposed to waiting until the entire submarine was raised to the surface, grew. Many of the dead sailors' families sided with safety.

On RTR television, the son of one of the crew members asked, "Why risk additional tragedies? Why deprive those divers' families of fathers, as happened in this case?" *Komsomolskaya Pravda* printed an editorial on the Navy tradition of a sunken ship being the crew's grave.

The dispute became a moral issue. In an open letter to

Putin, 78 relatives of the deceased *Kursk* crew asked that any recovery effort be postponed. They did not want any more men to "risk their lives."

In a way, the relatives' wish for a delay was granted. Talks between Rubin Design and Stolt had been abandoned. Rather than announce a termination of negotiations, signing of the contract was postponed indefinitely. This setback had the potential to delay the start date for entering the *Kursk*. So Deputy Prime Minister Klebanov convened a meeting of government officials and ordered Rubin to make a deal as quickly as possible. A list of eight firms capable of handling the complex job was made and discussions were scheduled with each of the organizations.

The controversy over the body-recovery program did have one distinct advantage. The furor helped cloak an important search activity taking place at the *Kursk*'s resting place.

26 September 2000

The *Akademik Mstislav Keldysh*, a scientific vessel belonging to the Russian Academy of Sciences' Institute of Oceanology, is registered in the port of Kaliningrad. The *Keldysh* has been operating for two decades and had made 45 scientific expeditions in 17 areas of the world's oceans.

Developed for marine studies, the *Keldysh* has a number of capabilities. One is its role as mother ship for two *Mir* deep-water submersibles. These football-shaped, orange and white submarines are propeller driven and fully self-contained. They are capable of operating in depths approaching 20,000 feet and can remain down for 15 hours. Equipment includes video recording, sonar detection, manipulator arms for collecting samples or fragments, and accommodations for passengers.

After an extended voyage from the North Atlantic, the *Keldysh* arrived at the *Kursk* disaster site. The Russian government was reported to have paid more than ten million dollars to hire the services of the vessel and its highly trained crew.

The mission was carefully detailed. The *Keldysh* would deploy the *Mir* craft. Then the mother ship and her minisubs would scour the path taken by the *Kursk* and the sea floor around the submarine itself. The goal was to find and retrieve debris that would prove or at least indicate a collision between the *Kursk* and a foreign boat. By combining a sonar search from the *Keldysh* and rigorous undersea hunting by the two *Mir* submersibles, the ocean bottom would be subjected to a foot-by-foot examination.

When Admiral Vladimir Valuyev, first deputy commander, Baltic Fleet, finally revealed the plan to reporters, he noted that when proof was found, "apart from moral liability, there will also be financial sanctions" against those responsible.

Mir-1 and *Mir-2* had experience working with submarines. During 1994 and 1995, the two submersibles had been used on the sunken *Komsomolets* nuclear sub. The task had been to install plugs in the torpedo hatches to prevent plutonium from leaching out of the atomic warheads into the water.

For five days at the *Kursk* site, one or the other or both of the craft were down. The exhausting undersea search required 95 hours of sustained drudgery. Using every instrument and capability, the small, tough craft crossed and recrossed each block of a meticulously laid out search zone.

An area equal to three square miles around the sunken *K-141*, plus a long swath following the *Kursk*'s final path, was inspected with the latest scientific equipment. Several metal fragments were collected and proved to be portions of the *Kursk*'s inner and outer hulls. Damage to the samples gave clear evidence of a tremendous onboard explosion originating in the *Kursk* torpedo room. The search revealed no indication of collision with another vessel.

The leader of the accident investigation commission, Klebanov, was to later state that experts no longer considered collision with another vessel to be the most likely cause of the tragedy. Evidently, the "experts" did not include many high-ranking Navy officers, who were far from ready to give up the collision theory. Building on the rumor of the earlier alleged secret conversation with President Clinton, a story was leaked: the *Mir* submersibles did discover debris from a U.S. sub. This "proof" had been suppressed in accordance with the supposed Putin-Clinton agreement.

2 October 2000

As the twin *Mir*s worked the seabed, Rubin Design was busy selecting the firm that would supply divers and equipment for entry into the *Kursk*. After extensive interviews and discussions of cost, a decision was made. The Russians signed a contract in St. Petersburg, with the fee reported to be $7 million. The chosen company's spokesperson explained that the low bid would be offset by the high profile of the operation. Rubin Design had hired Halliburton AS, a Norwegian subsidiary of an American energy services company.

With diving soon to begin, testing the water for radioactive materials intensified. The Norwegian Radiation Protection Authority noted no trace of contamination around the boat and they were set to evaluate samples from inside the hull when available. Since no radiation had been detected, there was confidence that all nuclear safety systems were working properly and the divers would not be endangered.

Halliburton delivered a world-class diving team. Don Degener, the only American selected for the *Kursk* job, in many ways typified the experienced diver. During a career that spanned almost three decades, he had worked on oil rigs and a variety of undersea construction projects.

To support the divers, Halliburton AS acquired the use of a platform ship, the *Regalia*. It is a bit strange to call the *Regalia* a ship even though it is a self-powered vessel that has a sea crew of sailors. The *Regalia* looks more like a massive, block-square, floating construction site, complete with metal buildings, a helipad, derricks, cranes, and other equipment. Built expressly for the purpose of serving offshore industries, the *Regalia* is an ideal mother ship. It can handle 18 saturation divers in three pressure chambers, each of which accommodates six men. There are two diving bells, both with three-man capacity. Built in Sweden during 1985, the *Regalia* was designed as what is known as a "semisubmersible" platform, with deep pontoonlike hulls extending down into the water. It is extremely stable and capable of continuing operations in rough weather and high seas.

When Degener arrived, he became part of an 18-man team that consisted of one South African, a Norwegian, and nine British divers. They would soon be joined by the six Russians who were completing their training in St. Petersburg.

On Monday, October 9, 2000, the *Regalia* sailed for Honningsvag, Norway, to collect special equipment.

During early contract negotiations, Halliburton AS engineers had studied the best method of cutting through the *Kursk* hulls. Slicing the thick steel would be difficult enough working in a shipyard dry dock. Doing it underwater made the job far more demanding and dangerous. To further complicate matters, long-term forecasts placed the likelihood of violent storms at almost 100 percent.

After reviewing their options, the technical staff contacted Oil States MCS, Ltd., in England, a firm that provides a unique abrasive water-jet cutting system. The process was originally developed as a means of severing undersea pilings and pipes. Advances in the technology allowed it to be used for cutting through flat as well as curved surfaces.

In the jet system, copper slag, a highly abrasive substance, is mixed with water and pumped through a high-pressure hose to the cutting head. The water jet would strike the metal to be cut with a force of more than 14,500 pounds per square inch.

Within days after the contract was awarded, the system was given a six-hour test. A robotic control device was attached to a steel plate similar to the *Kursk* hull. The cutting head was then locked on to the robot arm, which allowed the system operator to direct the cutter's movement as the cut progressed. The trial proceeded smoothly. An enthusiastic team packed the equipment in portable buildings similar to cargo containers. These modules were then trucked to Honningsvag and loaded onto the *Regalia.*

Cruising at a stately six knots, the *Regalia* then set out for the salvage site. While the *Regalia* plowed her way through the icy waves, a series of seemingly random events occurred. Examined one at a time, these incidents do not seem connected. Taken as a whole, they reveal a picture of Russia and the confusion that was engulfing the country.

The Navy high command had decided to boost morale and at the same time display the value of the Navy to the defense of Russia. So on October 11, ceremonies were held to celebrate the 300th anniversary of the founding of the Russian Navy. The public display of honoring past naval heroes generated some interest from the news media. But the event was not the hoped-for success because, in the midst of the celebration, Admiral Vladimir Kuroyedov, head of the Russian Navy, again stated his intention to resign. He also took full responsibility for the *Kursk* catastrophe. The *Kursk*'s dark shadow dimmed the festivities. Reality collided with rhetoric, and reality won.

Next, on Friday, October 13, Ilya Klebanov, the deputy prime minister heading the *Kursk* investigation, formally announced the *Mir* sea-floor search had found nothing, and a collision with another submarine was not the most likely cause of the disaster. That single statement began to unravel the collision theory.

The final event in this period occurred on October 19,

when a letter from Irina Lyachina, widow of Gennadi Lyachin, the *Kursk* commander, appeared in *Komsomolskaya Pravda*. She accused Murmansk regional authorities of misusing money collected to aid families of *Kursk* crewmen. And she resigned her position on the commission's board. In the aftermath, the Murmansk regional governor froze the bank accounts and called for a government audit. President Putin, who must have been wondering if the entire *Kursk* mess would ever fade away, ordered the deputy prime minister in charge of social services to investigate.

If nothing else, these happenings, along with constant statements from ranking Navy officers that the body-recovery attempt would be stopped if it became overly dangerous, indicated Russian military and political leadership were in turmoil.

20 October 2000—The Kursk Site

The *Peter the Great* was slowly working a grid pattern, cruising back and forth across the sea on patrol. The practice of dropping depth charges and hand grenades to ward off unwelcome sub-sea interlopers who might be attempting to enter the wreck had continued. In the cruiser's wake there were explosions that blew columns of water high into the sky. As the *Regalia* approached the area, those on board could see the white geysers and hear the hollow booms made by the explosives.

For October, the seas were reasonably calm. The weather window, however, was closing. Violent storms were on the way and it was feared a combination of wind and waves would make it impossible for the diver-support ship to hold position, forcing work to stop and the entire mission to be abandoned.

Utilizing satellite navigation aids, the *Regalia* was located over the wreck. The ship hovered over the spot on the bottom, 353 feet below, using the power of its thruster-propeller system.

Shortly after the *Regalia*'s arrival, relatives of the lost submariners, civilian dignitaries, and naval officers had come on board. A brief memorial service was held to honor the dead.

In anticipation of beginning work quickly, video and radiation-monitoring devices were lowered to the sunken boat so the divers could study conditions. Even with underwater visibility somewhat limited, the first looks at the sub were awe inspiring. Under bright camera lights the huge shape loomed out of the darkness like a goliath in a Mesozoic sea.

The visual survey completed, plans were laid for making the first cut. And the divers completed their pressurized saturation of the oxygen-helium gas mixture they would be breathing for the coming weeks.

Using Rubin Design's wire templates, decisions were made on how and precisely where to anchor the cutting nozzle and manipulator arm onto the sub's outer skin. With all equipment inspected and approved, it was time to begin. Work was once more going to continue on a 24-hour basis.

The first crew of three divers went through the airlock from the pressurized habitat into the cramped diving bell. The trio was lowered to the bottom, where one, as usual, remained inside the bell to monitor air, communications links, and heated water supplies sent down from above.

The other two slithered out the open bottom and entered the ocean gloom.

Powerful lights on their helmets illuminated only a small portion of the sleek, curving hull. Resting level on the bottom, the *Kursk* towered five stories above them. As they floated next to the submarine at its approximate midpoint, their brilliant lamps could not penetrate the darkness enough to see the bow or stern. Severe destruction, however, was clearly visible on the forward portion of the sub.

They swam alongside the vessel, moving upward until the sail loomed into view and the damage was evident. The masts for periscopes, radar, and radio had been torn away. It was still possible to wiggle into the enclosed lookout station where Captain Lyachin had stood before going to sea for the final time. As they glided back down again, close to the bottom, "marine snow" or fine silt was churned up from the seabed, which reduced vision even more.

Working in practiced unison, the crew rigged racks of floodlights lowered from the *Regalia* to illuminate their operations area. Following the dive plan and using instructions from above to assist them, they located a maintenance hatch. Inside, they singled out the line leading to the compressed air tanks. Severing that pipe would be their first challenge.

Next, they painstakingly fitted the robot that would hold and control the cutting system. Their lifeline umbilicals, extending 65 feet behind each of them to the bell, also contained a return line to recycle the expensive helium-oxygen breathing gas called heliox, so it could be used again.

The men were experienced at getting the most accomplished from every moment of bottom time. Their motions had the appearance of a strange ballet. Each understood it was better to do a task once, no matter how slowly, than to rush, make mistakes, and have to repeat an action.

The tools the divers employed had been specially modified for use in hands encumbered by wetsuit gloves. Even the simplest act of threading a bolt into a hole demanded exaggerated care. And like space walkers in zero gravity, correct body placement was required to exert any leverage on a wrench.

Pressure on their bodies at this depth was ten times that at sea level. Nevertheless, these men, who had spent years learning and perfecting the skills that allowed them to work in the deep, were calm and deliberate. They knew the diver's most important truth: mistakes on their part were the biggest danger they faced. If a life-threatening problem occurred, it would most likely arise because of their own errors. Do it once, do it right, and don't foul up. Those were words they lived by.

CHAPTER 11

21 October 2000—Aboard the Regalia

THE EXPANSIVE PLATFORM HAD ALMOST 11,000 SQUARE yards of space filled with marine construction and oil-well work-over equipment. Here and there, steel-sided, windowless office buildings jutted upward several stories high. The *Regalia* was a floating, made-to-order city that never slept.

In a low prefab portable building, constructed on skids and lashed to the deck, Oil States MCS engineer Nick Jones and a technician had readied their system. A bank of television monitors delivered real-time color pictures from below.

The first cuts were to be made for safety purposes. The divers had located and opened a hatch in the superstruc-ture. Inside was access to a thick pipe that conducted compressed air from the storage tank to the water ballast compartment. Severing this key pipe would allow any re-maining air pressure to blow into the ocean.

The divers affixed the cutter's robot control, cutting head, and video camera to the pipe. After ensuring proper placement at the correct angle, the engineer was ready to begin. The divers, who were visible on one TV screen, moved away from the work area. The powerful jet, as one man put it, could "cut your leg off like a light saber out of *Star Wars.*"

Turning the system on was almost anticlimactic. For a moment, it seemed nothing had happened. There was no sound, no brilliant flash of light from a cutting torch. Seconds passed, then minutes. Suddenly the technician reversed his controls. Trapped air violently spewed from the partially cut pipe. Quickly, the line was completely severed. They had gained access to the air chamber and it was almost completely flooded. Everyone was relieved.

Following instructions, the divers moved to the next hatch and airline. Then, working at the same deliberate pace, they disassembled the cutting system and transferred it to that site. The tear-down and setup took time, but making certain the air ballast chambers were inert could save a diver's life.

While working, the two divers watched each other for signs of "high pressure nervous syndrome." Individuals who remained below 300 feet for a full shift while breathing the heliox mixture might suddenly develop trembling or other neurological complications that could become incapacitating.

After four hours of grueling undersea activity, the first diving team's shift was up. Another trio descended in the second bell and two exhausted men made their way back to their sea-floor retreat. On the way up to the surface airlock that would allow them to enter their pressurized habitat, they sat shivering in their seats. Helium in their breathing gas conducts heat rapidly, which chills those who breathe it despite the circulating hot water in their suits.

By the end of the second shift, the divers had completed venting the compressed air ballast system tanks and were ready to begin the real work of making man-sized entry openings into the submarine.

22 October 2000—The Kursk Site

The divers now confronted a different challenge. The outside of the submarine was coated with a three-plus-inch layer of rubberlike elastomer to deaden sound and reduce surface friction while running at speed. This was bonded to the outer hull or superstructure, which was built from steel plate more than a third of an inch thick.

Cutting through the elastomer proved more difficult than predicted. In an earlier test, the "rubber" material had been dense. On the *Kursk*, only the top three-quarters of an inch was solid. Beneath that, the substance was honeycombed, which reduced cutting efficiency. The polymer outer coating was going to be a larger obstacle than envisioned, so a planning session was held to develop a strategy.

It was decided to make two cuts at an angle to the surface. This would create a V-shaped incision through the tough elastomer, almost down to metal. The divers, working with hydraulic chisels, would remove the V-section and then clear away the rest of the material to expose the steel. After fitting the wire Rubin Design template to locate the spot for the first hole, they began to cut.

This system worked and progress was excellent. With metal now exposed, the robotic arm was repositioned. When that task was completed, the first penetration of the superstructure or outer hull was set to begin.

The program called for cutting five circular openings through the outer hull to give the divers ample access. Each hole would be about four feet in diameter. After an opening was complete, a pair would enter the space between the outer and inner hulls to clear away piping, various obstructions, and cable. Uncluttered space would permit the cutting system to be transferred to the thicker pressure hull to make four more apertures. Crews handling the cutting system were also charged with slicing samples from the outer hull for later study. It was hoped these "coupons" would provide clues to the cause of the accident.

As an added safety measure, a preliminary hole, about six inches in diameter, would be made in the inner hull. A tiny video camera would be inserted into the sub's interior for a visual inspection prior to entry. Then checks for radioactivity and water content would be completed as well.

Work progressed rapidly and expectations were high. The operation was ahead of schedule and all would be well if the weather held. It didn't.

23–24 October 2000—The Kursk Site

A northwest wind that had been intensifying during the day built to gale force as evening approached. Waves increased to 35 feet, and the crews on the small fleet of ships prepared for a real blow. As the storm worsened, there was concern that the *Regalia* might be unable to maintain its position in the water, compromising the mission and risking the divers' lives. On October 23 at 1715 hours, an emergency call went down to the men on the bottom. They evacuated to the diving bell and were returned to their habitat on board the *Regalia*.

Storms in the Arctic have a tendency to settle over an area and wreak havoc for days. This one was no exception. With everyone out of the water, space inside the pressure chambers was tight. Each man had a bunk, which left little floor space.

Since most of the diving crew were exhausted from their underwater activities, napping helped keep boredom at bay. Sufficient rest, however, opened the door to low spirits. Every minute that passed with nothing done took them further from their goal. Eight hours was enough. By 0145 hours on October 24 a team was back on the bottom. Conditions were abysmal. Bottom silt limited their vision and there was the ever present danger of suddenly being jerked backward and thrown down by the umbilical cord being dragged in a sudden motion of the ship. The divers lasted just over an hour before being forced to return topside to the *Regalia*.

Toward what passed for dawn in the high regions, wind lessened and wave heights decreased. The platform ship was once more inside its operational limits and could accurately hold station. As soon as the sea crew repositioned her, the men returned to work.

The underwater team had developed a system for this job. Each circular opening in the outer hull, after the polymer was chiseled away, required about an hour to cut. When a hole was completed, ragged metal edges

were smoothed to prevent ripping a pressure suit or umbilical. For further protection, the entire perimeter of an
entryway was cushioned with a rubberized collar.

Then a cleanup crew went inside the space between
the double hulls to clear working room. They removed an
astonishing array of pipes, tanks, structural supports, and
control mechanisms. This task required major surgery
with shears and cutting torches because the designers had
filled the area to capacity to reduce clutter inside the pressure hull. Once a sufficient expanse was opened, another
team set the Rubin-produced templates as cutting patterns on the inside hull.

To be certain those templates were accurate, Rubin
Design engineers had checked their projections on a sister boat of the *Kursk*. Evidently, not all the giant subs
were built to exactly the same dimensions. One of the
patterns indicated cutting at a bulkhead joint. Metal in
this spot was several times thicker than in other places
because the boat had been made in sections or compartments that extended from bulkhead to bulkhead.

The divers ran into further difficulty when one of the
surfaces to be cut was curved as opposed to flat. Improvising, the divers remained at the cutting site, continu-
ously adjusting space between the cutting nozzle and the
hull by hand. With water impeding every movement,
alignment required diligence on the part of the dive team.

While the divers were methodically performing minor
miracles down below, politics crept into the recovery project on the surface. In what can only be described as a
contrived photo-op event, Russian Navy Chief Vladimir
Kuroyedov flew to the site. His mission was to cancel the
operation if he felt the divers' lives might be imperiled in

the search for bodies. His public stance served to support the notion that body retrieval was the main purpose of this activity. The admiral was accompanied by two widows of lost *Kursk* crew members who cast flowers into the waters and presented home-baked pies to the *Regalia* team.

Kuroyedov did not stop the project. So shortly before midnight, after hours of hard labor, the first diver-access port through the pressure hull was completed. Now they could enter the eighth compartment. As was customary, a video scan of the inside had been made to locate any potential hazards prior to sending in a diver. Although camera range was limited due to visibility, the area around the new entrance seemed clear of obstacles.

24–25 October 2000

Large batteries of lights were set in place to illuminate the opening. Then, as per the dive plan, Russians relieved their non-Russian counterparts. At 1500 hours a Navy diver swam to the portal. He was quickly joined by another man who would provide support.

It had taken a huge effort to gain access to the *Kursk*'s interior. Now the way was open. Without hesitation the Russian edged into the newly cut hole and slid inside the dark tomb. Moving about required considerable care because of the massive amount of debris cluttering all available space.

Water in the compartment was cloudy with silt. Neither the helmet light nor his high-intensity handheld lamp could dispel the gloom. At times, according to reports, visibility was down to inches.

Swimming cautiously, the diver began an examination of the boat's interior. Video images he relayed to the surface showed traces of a massive fire and damage caused by impact with the sea bottom. A running commentary supported the pictures he sent.

The full nature of this first diver's assignment inside the *Kursk* is not known. It is logical, however, to assume that part of his duties were exploratory. By providing an accurate account of conditions, he was establishing parameters for planning subsequent onboard activities.

As the diver moved toward the vessel's rear sections, the lack of human remains must have seemed strange. Even though the *Kursk* was a huge, multilevel submarine and visibility was limited, there had been 118 people on board. Not all would have been destroyed by the blast or immolated in the blazing aftermath. So finding the first body must have been both a shock and a relief. The subsequent discovery of three more fallen comrades most likely generated a sense of sadness. As part of his training, he'd been told to avoid looking at the faces of the dead men. That was good advice, but impossible to follow.

Cold and salt water had preserved the bodies. The many days under pressure from the sea had given them zero buoyancy. They remained static, floating in place until shifted by an eddy or current. This weightlessness made moving the remains through the jumbled interior of the boat a relatively easy task. Considering adverse conditions, three bodies were retrieved in a relatively short period of time. The fourth corpse was trapped behind a mass of rubble and would require further work to collect.

Special containers were lowered from the surface and each body was placed in one of the sealable units. They would be airlifted to the naval hospital in Severomorsk. There, the Laboratory of Judicial and Medical Examination, Unit Number 1082, waited to perform autopsies and other tests on the remains.

To aid the divers, six psychologists had been brought on board as part of the recovery group. Now that remains were being recovered, their services might be in demand.

25–26 October 2000

Work inside the *Kursk* intensified. A pair of men had been sent to recover the fourth body. They labored under difficult conditions and had to be careful not to become entangled in the debris. Adding to their strain was news of more foul weather. It was anticipated the gale on the way would be worse than its predecessor. So as a safety precaution all divers were about to be recalled to the *Regalia*. The recovery team chose to continue their operation. Two hours were required to free the fourth corpse and more time was needed to pack the body into its container and lift it to the surface.

While work on the bottom was curtailed, engineers were able to refine their program. Opening the main hatch between the eighth and seventh compartments became the next priority. Templates were selected to cut an entry port into Compartment 7. As soon as conditions improved, clear water would be pumped into Compartment 9 in order to flush out enough mud and improve visibility. In the meantime, all they could do was wait for good weather.

CHAPTER 12

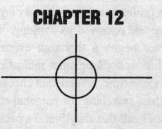

26 October 2000—Aboard the Regalia

THE STORM THAT STRAFED THE *REGALIA* WITH HAIL AND high winds intensified as the day progressed. Recovery efforts were paralyzed, a planned memorial service was postponed, and all flight operations were canceled. So it was impossible to transport the retrieved bodies to the Vidyaevo Navy hospital. The remains of the four crewmen were placed in the *Regalia*'s sick bay. The ship had provisions for first-rate medical care. Even though the vessel was better equipped to handle industrial accidents as opposed to postmortems, the facilities were more than adequate.

Since the intent had been to fly the bodies to shore, the Russian hospital ship that had been standing by in port was not part of the salvage flotilla. There were, however, qualified Russian forensics specialists serving as part of *Regalia*'s company. Termination of flight ac-

tivities did not necessarily mean having to wait to identify the bodies.

In the infirmary, standard military practice was followed. There was no apparent need for secrecy, so the infirmary area was not off-limits to ship personnel.
Working with professional coolness, a corpsman laid out
the first corpse and removed its clothing. With that completed, a doctor began a thorough examination of the
body for visible wounds or other indications of trauma.
At almost the same time, an assistant checked through the
seaman's clothes, searching for personal effects.

The man assigned that duty found a packet wrapped in
plastic in a breast pocket. Opening it, he removed several
handwritten pages. The edges were charred and the oil-
stained paper damp, but the writing was legible. Dmitry
Kolesnikov's carefully scribed notes had returned to the
land of the living. And they were discovered in front of
several non-Russians assisting or watching the physi-
cians work.

Many experts believe that if Dmitry's note had been
uncovered in the naval hospital at Vidyaevo, its very existence would have been suppressed. Outside of need-to-
know officials, chances are that no one, including
Dmitry's family, would have learned of its existence.

Several people who read Russian saw one or more
pages before they vanished into the sealed archives of the
commission investigating the disaster. So it was impossible for the government or military to deny that a note existed. From the standpoint of damage control, the best
that could be done was to keep possession of the letter
and publicly reveal as little as possible. So when the note

was dispatched to shore, it was claimed by military prosecutors and classified Top Secret.

Reports of Dmitry's final letter reached the news media which forced the Navy to officially announce its discovery. Subsequent leaks allowed part of the text to appear in print. This disclosure caused his parents and wife to begin an active campaign to see the note. The event revived public indignation and brought new accusations of a deliberate slow start to the emergency rescue effort as well as rejection of official statements on the cause of the sinking.

In an attempt to counter the groundswell, what was supposed to be the "full text" of the note was read on national television. The letter emphasized a timeline that strongly indicated the men trapped in the ninth compartment had come to a speedy end. The new official revelations were met with disbelief. Many publicly argued that the "full text" had been severely edited.

A number of leaks purporting to reveal additional content appeared in the press. One of the most damning was a report attributed to the Moscow newspaper *Zhizn*. In the story, one I. O. Griaznov, a military expert from the Severomorsk laboratory, allegedly stated that there was a second note found in Dmitry's pocket, written on Tuesday, August 15, three days after the sinking. That message supposedly included: "Captain died . . . I am the only chief officer left on board. . . . It hurts . . . Murdered . . . August 15th."

The August 15 date was a matter of great consternation because it meant that if a Deep Sea Rescue Vehicle had been able to mate with the escape hatch, there might have been survivors. Northern Fleet officers quickly labeled the Griaznov text a fake.

Dmitry's father, Roman Kolesnikov, believed his son's military training would have come before sentiment. Therefore he was certain there must be unseen pages that recorded whatever information Dmitry had about the cause of the disaster and other technical matters. Based on his statements, Dmitry's first superior officer on the submarine, the ex-*Kursk* commander, agreed with Roman on this issue.

According to a report from Bellona, a science-based environmental organization, two copies of the note were made. One was supposedly for Northern Fleet Commander Admiral Popov. The second was said to have been for Dmitry's wife, Olga. She apparently did not receive it because *The Moscow Times* later reported that Dmitry's father was finally allowed to view the original note and make a personal copy. Dmitry's wife and mother, despite requests, had been unable to see it. Officials told them the note was being used in the investigation and would be given to them later.

The Russian military learned a costly lesson from this incident. In terms of maintaining prestige, respect, and dignity, it was better for them to control the news than respond to reports. All further work on the remains of *Kursk* submariners was carried out in private. When a second note was discovered, its release was handled in an entirely different manner.

An official announcement of the second note was slow in coming and pointedly did not provide the name of its author. Speculation among the families of those killed in the catastrophe was that it had been penned by Dmitry's best friend, Captain-Lieutenant Rashid Ariapov. According to a report in *Pravda*, the Northern Fleet deputy commander verified this to the officer's family.

No relatives have been allowed to see this missive and the limited text released for publication was of a technical nature. The comments included a reference to what may be a shortage of the belts used in individual breathing kits and a lack of oxygen-regeneration units. Other quotes include: "Our condition is bad. We have been weakened by the effects of carbon monoxide. Pressure is increasing. We can't make it more than 24 hours."

What else the note revealed is a matter of conjecture.

27–31 October 2000—Aboard the Regalia

The storm raged all day Friday without slacking. With operations held in abeyance, there was little for anyone to do except prep equipment and wait for better weather.

The divers remained in their pressurized habitats so as to be able to start work again as quickly as possible. They knew the *Regalia* had only been rented for a set number of days and that time lost to inclement weather hurt the operation.

Discovery of the first bodies and the note indicating survivors had gathered in Compartment 9 made the Navy revise previous plans. They would continue efforts to cut into Compartment 7. At the same time, Russians, with longer umbilical lines, would take the previously explored route through Compartment 8 deep into the ninth. They would be supported by running a suction hose into the compartment from a dredge barge on the surface. It was hoped that drawing out the muddy water and replacing it with clear seawater would improve visibility.

At 0400 hours on the morning of October 28, the divers went down again. The Russian team entered the watery hell of the ninth compartment. Visibility was only slightly improved. Much of the searching had to be done by moving arms and hands before them as they advanced. Hampered by their long umbilicals, they began a painstaking exploration of the area. If Dmitry's note was correct, many more bodies were waiting to be found in this section.

In a terrifying world not envisioned by Dante or Edgar Allan Poe, the Russians worked out a search system. Handicapped by debris unseen until they collided with it, they sought and found corpse after corpse. The grisly work went on, day in and day out, until an end was called at 1100 hours on October 31. Further searching had become too dangerous for the men to continue. Eight bodies had been recovered. They knew more were there, but conditions were so deplorable that a thorough search was ruled impossible.

20–30 October 2000—Mainland

While the divers continued operations in the *Kursk*, stories of the families of the deceased submariners began to appear in the news.

It was estimated that the average *Kursk* family would receive a little less than $40,000, which exchanged into just over 1,100,000 rubles. That's enough money in Russia, where monthly salaries can be 500 rubles, to be considered well off, if not rich. In 1999, an average salary was 1700 rubles ($60) per month. Contributions to funds set up for *Kursk* relatives totaled $4.2 million (118 million rubles). For 118 families that would be a million rubles (about $36,000) each and this was only October.

One mother, from a collective farm in the Ural Mountains, returned home to find her job had been taken. People thought she wouldn't want to work now that she was wealthy. The woman managed to regain her position, but when payday came, she received nothing. They thought she no longer needed to be paid. Her 14-year-old-daughter also had a hard time. Her classmates objected to the new clothes her mother purchased for her.

Her dead son's father had arrived while she was still at the Vidyaevo naval base. He'd been hiding from her for over ten years to avoid making child support payments and now demanded 25 percent of her compensation. Then she began receiving letters from people with her same last name, claiming to be relatives and asking for money.

By late October, snow covered the ground at her village of 300 people and temperatures were dropping. When the village boiler broke, the local administration just assumed she'd pay for the repair.

Across the width and breadth of the Russian Federation, loss of the *Kursk* and questions raised by that disaster remained items of daily regret and speculation. Every activity relating to the submarine was therefore newsworthy. So on Sunday, October 29, when the Navy held a memorial ceremony in the restricted town of Severomorsk, it was well covered. On that blustery, partly cloudy day, hundreds of people gathered at Courage Square in the heart of the small community. Mourners carried framed photos of the lost submariners and assumed places around the seafront plaza. Four armored personnel carriers, each topped with a casket draped in the white and blue Navy flag, rumbled slowly into sight. Progressing at walking speed, the procession passed row upon row of officers and men. As the caskets rolled by, sailors removed their hats, bowed their heads, and dropped to one knee in the snow that covered the ground of this Arctic outpost.

When the procession stopped, all came to attention. One by one, the names of the 118 submariners who perished were read from a roll of honor. Mothers and fathers, hearing the name of their son, broke into tears.

Olga, Dmitry's beloved Olechka, was stiff with grief. Chin lifted and with fists clenched, she stared straight into the wind at the cold sun riding low on the horizon. Her life with Dmitry was finished. For her it was time to start over.

In the harbor, warships riding at anchor, guns and electronic antenna giving the sleek vessels a deadly air, blasted low, mournful horns in a farewell salute. In the final tribute, she could almost hear his voice. "I could drown in your eyes, like a real submariner, without any sound."

1–7 November 2000—Aboard the Regalia

A change now occurred in the recovery operation. Focus was shifted to the third compartment, where 24 crewmen had been posted. This was the communications center of the boat. If coding equipment and related items remained in salvageable condition, they would be found here. That area also had a shaft used in radio transmitting that was large enough to have sheltered a few people. And since there was a direct access to Compartment 2, which contained an escape capsule hatch, survivors might have gathered there, as well. Some Northern Fleet officials were also of the opinion that crew from Compartments 4 and 5 could have gone forward on their way to the escape route in Compartment 2.

A six- to seven-inch hole was cut into Compartment 3 and a TV recon started. Visibility was poor but what could be seen was extensive damage from both fire and explosive shock. By some reports, the conditions in Compartment 3 precluded divers from entering that space. There is eyewitness testimony, however, that one or more divers inspected or entered the submarine through the gaping hole blown in the forward hull.

The mission was running low on time. Every minute needed to be productive. In a spirit of cooperation, the divers agreed to stretch their work periods from four hours to six hours. An entry port was cut through the hull and the dredge pipe used to help clear the murky water. Despite reports to the contrary, Russian divers then went into Compartment 3. Intelligence materials in there were too valuable to be ignored.

The damage in the compartment excluded the possibility that anyone reached the escape hatch in the command center next door. Entire bulkheads had been blown away, leaving shards of broken, melted metal. Items from the second and third compartments were thrown together in a tangled mess. It was apparent in the first moments after entry that no bodies would be found. Body parts might exist amid the jumbled ruins or beneath the silt that covered the deck, but there was no way to tell.

None of the divers had arrived on-site with a complete understanding of how devastating the explosion on board the *Kursk* had been. As the extent of damage became known, a degree of discouragement began to replace optimism. It was obvious the fore part of the submarine was totally ravaged. Attention was focused now on the fourth compartment. One of the largest areas on the boat, Compartment 4 contained the cabins, galley, gym, sauna, and other crew facilities. A total of 12 men would have been stationed here during a battle stations drill.

As preparations were made to cut another entryway, a team of Russian divers was sent to take up-close video images of the mutilated area toward the bow. And in hopes of finding collision evidence, one more sea-floor reconnaissance was also conducted. Once again, nothing was discovered.

On November 3, storm conditions returned, halting work because of strong winds and blowing snow. When the weather improved, a research ship, the *Horizont*, arrived as a replacement for the *Semyon Dezhnyov*. These vessels were responsible for a continuous monitoring of the sea for radiation.

By Sunday, November 5, a Russian diver gained entrance to Compartment 4. Visibility was bad even though the area had been flushed to remove silt. As expected, conditions in the compartment were conclusive proof that the shock wave had smashed through, causing almost unimaginable damage. The bulkhead and watertight door between the fourth and fifth compartments somehow held. Because of the debris and the horrendous force of the blast, bodies were not expected to be found.

A clear picture of the mutilated sub was now evident. Every compartment had been ripped by a fire storm. Reactor safeguards had functioned as planned. No source on the boat was leaking radioactivity. The entire front half of the sub was a useless mass of melted, distorted metal. Only the crew shielded by the reinforced barriers of the reactor section could possibly have survived any length of time.

Every movement made by a diver working inside the burned-out hulk was fraught with danger. Some records, hull samples, and other materials were recovered. But there was not much more to be learned by further investigation.

Early on the morning of Tuesday, November 7, representatives from Rubin Design met on board the *Regalia* to discuss entry into Compartment 5. Although it was conceivable that some bodies might possibly be found on lower decks, limited reconnaissance provided a strong indication that many of the narrower passageways were blocked. So even though Halliburton's contract ran through November 10, the decision was made to cease operations. Orders were given, and the project was phased out.

The final act of the exhausting 18-day activity was the sealing of holes that had been cut through the hulls. The mission was over. Twelve bodies had been recovered and returned to Russia.

Early in the afternoon, a memorial service was attended by expedition personnel and members of the Russian Navy. A somber group ignored the foul weather and gathered on the deck of the platform ship. All present, regardless of nationality or allegiance, shared a deep sense of loss. Men who go down to the sea in ships form a brotherhood. Those who venture under the waves are brave and enjoy a special camaraderie. The loss felt in that final hour before parting brought tears to the eyes of the men who had lived with this tragedy. At about 1400 hours, the *Regalia*, with a long salute of its ship's horn, began its return to Norway.

CHAPTER 13

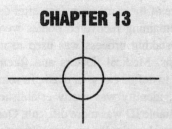

*1 November 2000–31 March 2001—
Russian Federation*

ALTHOUGH WORK AT THE RECOVERY SITE HAD COME TO A
close, popular interest in the disaster grew even stronger.
The Russian people hungered to know why the *Kursk* had
sunk and who or what was to blame. Publicly asking
those questions was an ideal way to demonstrate a new-
found freedom of expression. And demanding answers
gave the citizens an untried level of empowerment.

Unfortunately, the continued publicity made it more
difficult to obtain facts. News reporters were seemingly
everywhere, interviewing anyone with an opinion about
what had happened. The constant barrage obscured the
voices of the few real experts, allowing every ridiculous
notion to be heard.

Those who had attempted to avoid full disclosure of
accident information wanted this attention to fade and
die. If the news media would only quiet down, time

would erase the severity of the disaster from the people's minds. It had always worked that way in Russia. This group hoped the impending memorial services, as well as impressive military funerals that played well on TV news, would bring a measure of closure. Surely the public would tire of the same story, day after day.

As the remaining recovered bodies were returned to land, a painstaking process was used to make positive identifications. Medical doctors and forensic scientists also worked to define cause of death. In some cases, such as Dmitry's, identity was easily established. In others, proving a reliable ID was more difficult. One seaman had a breathing mask melted to his face. Others were severely burned. By November 4, extensive work had allowed 10 of the 12 recovered bodies to be identified. Cause of death was simpler to define. High concentrations of carbon monoxide were present in tissue samples.

As the remains were released to the families, plans were laid for individual funerals. Dmitry was returned to his native St. Petersburg for burial. The funeral was held at Admiralty Hall of Dzherzhinsky Naval College, his alma mater. This former palace, known for its golden spire, is a city landmark.

Captain-Lieutenant Dmitry Kolesnikov was laid to final rest with full honors on Thursday, November 2, 2000. His was the first funeral for the submariners lost on the *Kursk*.

More than 3,000 friends, colleagues, officials, and dignitaries attended the memorial service. Columns in the building had been spiral-wrapped with ribbons, and flags adorned the walls. In Russian Orthodox tradition, the family—his stoic father; his mother, weeping silently; his widow, face serious; and his younger brother—sat beside the wood and zinc coffin. A guard of honor stood silently by. More than a thousand mourners, many in uniform, gravely filed past the closed, flag-covered casket to offer sympathy.

A picture of Dmitry was placed in front of the coffin above a large framed copy of the note he had scrawled while awaiting rescue or death. There were no speeches. The only voice was that of the priest who prayed to God for Dmitry's "warrior soul."

A funeral procession column was formed. Led by the honor guard, a long, solemn line marched from the hall. Outside, umbrellas blossomed, protecting some from the rain as they took part in the final cortege. Walking slowly through the cold streets, grim-faced naval officers and sailors ignored the drizzle. They were led by one man carrying the photo of Dmitry that bore a diagonal black ribbon across the lower left corner. The officer behind him held Dmitry's Order of Courage medal in his hands.

As a military band played somber music, his mother wept openly. During the burial service, Northern Fleet Commander Vyacheslav Popov stated, "His fate will become an example of serving the fatherland for everyone. I will teach the officers, sailors, and midshipmen of the Northern Fleet according to his example."

At a barked command, a rifle detail in full dress uniform came to attention. A second order brought them to port arms. A third shout and rifles snapped to shoulders. They fired in unison, paused, shot another volley, then a third into the air with military precision.

Olechka, Dmitry's beloved, who knew his last thoughts had been of her, stood with her body rigid as a stick. Proud of Dmitry and the tribute to his memory, it was clear she would trade all the high honors for one more moment with him alive, holding her. The poem he wrote before the *Kursk* sailed on its final voyage would remain with her always. "And when the time comes to die, though I chase such thoughts away, I want time to whisper one thing: 'My darling, I love you.' " She knew his last words had been for her.

Captain-Lieutenant Dmitry Kolesnikov was placed to rest in the section of Serafimovskoye Cemetery known as Hero's Way.

In another anguishing bit of irony, the remains of Viktor Kuznetsov, a senior midshipman who had been a turbine operator mate, were identified. Ill and tortured by waiting for news, his mother died in the city of *Kursk*. The family was notified that Viktor's body had been recovered only two hours after his mother had passed away. A pair of coffins were placed side by side for the service. His mother was buried in the city's southern cemetery while her son was interred in town near a memorial to those who perished in the Great Patriotic War (World War II).

These funerals, and those held for the others who had perished, dampened the spirits of many Russians. Coverage of the events, though, increased rather than decreased interest in the *Kursk* disaster.

The public seemed insatiable. The situation had become a nationwide affliction. And in spite of efforts to correct the problem, some Russian leaders were still at times operating at cross purposes. The friction caused by their lack of cohesion was the very ingredient that kept the story fresh in the public's eye.

Important people tend to appear foolish when they make a statement one day, then deny it the next. Demonstrations of such blunders were easy to find. No lesser a person than Deputy Prime Minister Klebanov gave a widely publicized announcement that a logbook had been recovered from the *Kursk*. According to a *Moscow Times* story, the news operation *Interfax* quoted Klebanov, in his capacity as head of the *Kursk* investigating commission, as stating, "We recovered what we could—certain notes and the logbook from the fourth compartment."

The next day, Tuesday, November 14, *The St. Petersburg Times* noted that Klebanov issued a press release saying the documents recovered earlier in the month from the *Kursk* did not include a logbook. Instead, only technical bits of documentation were retrieved and none of this material provided any new information on what had occurred.

Another error was evident from Klebanov's at times single-minded insistence on rallying any support possible for the collision theory. On November 8, reports indicated that as head of the Russian government panel, Klebanov stated the divers recovering bodies had found "serious visual evidence" of a collision between the *Kursk* and another sub. Then he noted that it was too early to give clear answers about what happened. This ploy of making a revelation based on speculation, then backing away from it without offering proof, appeared to have been strangely effective—as was the willingness to change positions on the collision issue with ease. In October, when there was no refuting that the two *Mir* submersibles had searched and found no evidence of collision, Klebanov explained that a collision was unlikely.

Such vacillation may have been an indication of an open mind confronting new evidence. Or, it's possible the changes could be attributed to backstage political tactics aimed at keeping others in line. The threat of forging a new alliance during a delicate time can be an effective way of holding on to an old ally.

Again and again, throughout the story of the *Kursk*, it seems a deliberate effort had been made to create confusion. Was this the case? Or was the Russian military and government leadership so disjointed they could not present a united front?

Since facts are the bane of confusion, offering facts will end much of the mystery. Use of fiction in place of truth only creates more discombobulation.

A prime example of such disorganization was the problem caused by unkept promises. A widely reported statement made on October 24 by the commander of the Russian Navy, Admiral Vladimir Kuroyedov, trumpeted his view of the cause of the *Kursk* sinking. "I am eighty percent sure it was a collision with another submarine. In the next two months, I will make up the other twenty percent and will announce to the world who it was."

A great deal more than two months have passed since that statement, and Admiral Kuroyedov has yet to make his announcement. He has, however, been quoted often in the media maintaining a collision did occur.

In short, there have been accusations, recriminations, and demands to inspect U.S. as well as other NATO nations' sub fleets. Everything but evidence of a collision has been offered. And not surprisingly, staunch denials have met almost every attempt to offer a noncollision scenario.

This iron-curtain defense has been sustained for months. A few rust spots, however, started to appear on the once shiny surface. On February 27, 2001, *The Moscow Times* focused attention on a story in the normally pro-government newspaper *Izvestia*. In the report, *Izvestia* stated that the second note found on a *Kursk* crewman blamed the explosion on an experimental torpedo.

The exploding torpedo concept gained more support from Igor Spassky, a member of the investigating commission and head of Rubin Central Design Bureau. Spassky reportedly hinted that a torpedo was the cause. Several days after the accident, a person referred to in Russian newspapers as the "mouthpiece" of the Defense Ministry commented that the sub had been refitted to carry new torpedoes that were "difficult to store and dangerous to handle." Then an admiral from the Northern Fleet jumped in with this published quote: "One cannot deny the possibility that during firing, the torpedo did not leave the hatch completely and exploded inside it."

Not surprisingly, Dagdizel, the torpedo designers, continued to be adamant about the safety of their weapons. During the months after the bodies were recovered, Dagdizel maintained a low-key presence.

The one line of blame for the accident that refuses to fade away and still has teeth is the persistent scenario in which a missile from the *Peter the Great* cruiser triggered the disaster.

In early March 2001, a retired Russian admiral, said to have been connected with the ill-fated rescue operation, reportedly agreed to be interviewed in the town of Murmansk. In a published article, he stated that documents concerning the *Kursk* were being hidden. He also indicated a launched Shipwreck missile from the cruiser went the wrong way. This missile purportedly hit the water near the *Kursk* with tremendous impact. This, in turn, caused the *Kursk* to roll and shudder sufficiently to dislodge a torpedo from its rack. The weapon then leaked its highly volatile fuel.

If that occurred, the leaking torpedo would have been loaded into a tube and shot away from the submarine as quickly as permission to fire was obtained from Fleet HQ.

This sequence of events certainly fits the known reports and accounts for the eyewitness comments. Even weapons experts who have expressed doubts about this explanation have, in fairness, said it is not impossible.

What really did sink the *Kursk*?

Will we ever know?

The answer to both questions is yes.

The real cause of the *Kursk* disaster is clear.

PART III
THE LESSON

WHAT REALLY SANK THE *KURSK*!

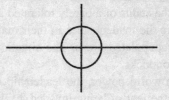

A single word defines the force that actually sank the *Kursk*.

That word is "attitude."

As history has proven, it is far easier to strive to regain old glories than accept new realities. In brief, that's the story of Russian military management since the fall of the Soviet Union.

Under the old regime, the Union of Soviet Socialist Republics attained a position of world power based solely upon its military might.

Behind that warrior shield, which was often made from smoke and mirrors, there was no infrastructure to support the nation's claim to greatness.

The Russian road system was abominable. Other means of transportation were inadequate. The agricultural capabilities were consistently unable to sustain the population. Russian manufacturing potential was far beneath the people's needs. Health-care facilities were marginal. Housing was substandard as well as crowded. Sanitation facilities were stressed to the maximum. And Russian educational efforts had become sorely limited.

Human rights were dismissed, and each individual became, in too real a sense, a ward of the state. So the family unit was placed in a secondary role and religion was relegated to the status of a barely tolerated anachronism.

These were the inadequacies in their major cities and most heavily populated areas. The situation was worse out in the boondocks.

To sustain world power, the leadership of the USSR played upon the fear of being invaded, utilized nationalism as a force to unify a diverse people as well as instill a distrust for foreigners, and hid the lifestyle deficiencies created by applying as much of the national productivity as possible to maintaining its military might.

Under Soviet control, the once proud scientific community was instructed to direct its internationally renowned capabilities to military purposes.

All art forms—in essence the nation's total creative effort—came under the watchful eye of government approval. It was also harnessed to pull the cart of nationalism.

And to ensure a positive image for the government among the people, continue support of military excesses, and sustain fear of foreign aggression, news sources were tightly controlled.

In short, the USSR was a nation in which the total possible output, aside from the barest essential needs of the populace, was devoted to maintaining a position of world importance through military strength. With this intense focus on arms and armaments, it was no wonder the highest echelon of military leaders gained and nurtured a degree of self-importance along with an attitude of arrogant superiority.

At the Soviet Union's demise, these leaders were, for the first time, faced with a rechanneling of national output because of a fresh positioning of government. In the new era of the Russian Federation, military needs, once the master, were relegated to a subservient status.

To claim that this was difficult for many to accept is an understatement of massive proportions.

The concept that military force was no longer the driving reason for the nation's existence was, to many in the officer corps, unthinkable, unendurable, and unwise.

Yet it happened.

To regain past glories, which is also to say previous funding levels, the military has actively carried on a campaign to rekindle public fears of foreign acts of aggression. The North Atlantic Treaty Organization (NATO) has been cast by some as a loaded cannon pointed at the heart of the motherland. And only the threat of quick and dire retaliation has kept that cannon from being fired. Others have engaged in open warfare against former Soviet Union citizenry now labeled "rebels."

The military has yet to find, however, the right appeal to the people that will result in a demand to return the nation's money box to rearmament needs.

A country that has based its place in the ranks of the world's greatest powers on the threat and strength of its military capabilities must continue to demonstrate those capabilities. In the case of Russia's Northern Fleet, the annual sea maneuvers were one such demonstration. The much vaunted Mediterranean cruise, to show the world Russia's level of sea power, was another.

Demonstration of military abilities is always a dangerous and expensive game. And the danger increases exponentially as the ability to adequately fund such activities declines.

Because of their intended use, modern weapons systems, no matter how diligent the designers, are unsafe. The task of the system is to deliver destructive force on a designated target. To accomplish that goal, the system itself must contain the force to be delivered. And that force, regardless of the number of fail-safe checks imposed, is capable of self-ignition.

Due to this inherent destructive ability, the safe handling and firing of modern weapons systems requires extensive early training followed by constant practice with live ammunition and/or warheads. Allowing budgetary constraints to shorten the initial training or reduce practice time or dictate use of weaponry with less than the maximum available safety checks is a prelude to catastrophe.

To short safety in a period of depleted budgets and then demand performance equal or superior to that attained during times of sufficient funding is dancing with disaster.

The Russian bear, led by the military and especially the Navy, did that dance. And the *Kursk* disaster paid the fiddler.

It is easier, and probably more satisfying, to strive to regain old glories than accept new realities.

That attitude sank the *Kursk*.

That posture will continue to plague what can become a great nation on its considerable merits as opposed to lost military might.

EPILOGUE

MORE THAN A YEAR HAS PASSED SINCE THE SINKING OF THE *Kursk*. And the story is still making headlines.

Worldwide interest was rekindled in late summer and early fall of 2001 with the commencement of a long-promised operation to raise the lost submarine.

First statements about bringing up the *Kursk* indicated the purpose was to return the bodies of the lost seamen to their families. In practice, another goal, salvaging the boat's center and tail sections to recover the nuclear reactors and missiles, appears to have gained equal importance.

The bow segment, where the explosions occurred, and where there is reportedly recognizable missile damage, has been sliced off and left behind. Supposedly the Navy will retrieve it "at a later date." This is doubly strange because without careful examination of the bow segment there is no hope of defining what caused the disaster. And that knowledge is important to the future operation of other Russian submarines. As an aside, one story indicates that the cut to sever the bow from the rest of the boat was to be made at the point on the hull that was identified in a report as being the missile's point of impact.

To defend leaving the bow section, official concerns over the possibility of unexploded torpedoes were revealed. This is a strange position: first, because divers have explored the bow space, and undoubtedly political and military officials know what is inside. So there is no need for supposition about "possible" unexploded torpedoes. And second, had there been any real fear of another explosion, the mission to enter the sunken submarine in October 2000, to search for bodies, would never have taken place. Even one unexploded torpedo would have endangered the small flotilla at the disaster site and the divers cutting entry holes through the hulls. No mention was made then of such a potential hazard.

None of this is to imply that the recovery of the nuclear reactors and weapons is not beneficial. The cleanup is both necessary and prudent. For the Russians, it also reduces the opportunity for foreign intelligence missions to examine those items.

One final interesting fact has been revealed. Igor Spassky, head academician of the Rubin Central Design Bureau, was quoted in an article in *Itar-Tass* as stating that Russia is developing a fourth-generation submarine. And the forces that destroyed the *Kursk* are being considered in mapping its new design. From that comment, it is difficult not to believe that those in charge, despite statements about being unsure, know exactly what went wrong in those final, fatal moments.

In closing, it is appropriate to express sincere condolences to the families who lost loved ones in this tragic catastrophe—and to honor those who perished by including their names in this book.

CREW MEMBERS

Compartment 1

1. Senior Warrant Officer Abdulkadyr ILDAROV—torpedo crew petty officer (Dagestan Rep.)
2. Warrant Officer Aleksey ZUBOV—sonar group technician (Ukraine)
3. Seaman Ivan NEFEDKOV—torpedo section commander (Sverdlovsk Reg.)
4. Seaman Maxim BORZHOV—torpedoman (Vladimir Reg.)
5. Seaman Aleksey SHULGIN—bilge mechanic (Arkhangelsk Reg.)
6. Senior Lieutenant Arnold BORISOV—representative from the Dagdizel Plant (not a member of the crew) (Dagestan Rep.)
7. Mamed GADZHIYEV—representative from the Dagdizel Plant (not a member of the crew) (Dagestan Rep.)

Compartment 2

7th Submarine Division Headquarters
 1. Captain (1st Rank) Vladimir BAGRYANTSEV—chief of 7th Submarine Division Staff (Crimea Rep.)
 2. Captain (2nd Rank) Yury SHEPETNOV—missile flag officer (Crimea Rep.)
 3. Captain (2nd Rank) Viktor BELOGUN—electromechanical service deputy chief (Ukraine)
 4. Captain (2nd Rank) Vasily ISAYENKO—electromechanical group assistant to chief (Crimea Rep.)
 5. Captain (3rd Rank) Marat BAIGARIN—temporary acting torpedo flag officer (St. Petersburg)

Crew
 6. Captain (1st Rank) Gennadi LYACHIN—*Kursk* commander (Volgograd Reg.)
 7. Captain (2nd Rank) Sergey DUDKO—first officer (Byelorussia)
 8. Captain (2nd Rank) Alexander SHUBIN—deputy commander for training (Crimea Rep.)
 9. Captain-Lieutenant Maxim SAFONOV—navigation officer (Moscow Reg.)
10. Senior Lieutenant Sergey TYLIK—electrical navigation group commander (Murmansk Reg.)
11. Senior Lieutenant Vadim BUBNIV—electrical navigation group engineer (Ulyanovsk Reg.)
12. Captain (3rd Rank) Andrey SILOGAVA—missile officer (Crimea Rep.)
13. Captain-Lieutenant Aleksey SHEVCHUK—control party of missile department commander (Murmansk Reg.)
14. Senior Lieutenant Andrey PANARIN—control party of missile department engineer (Leningrad Reg.)

15. Senior Lieutenant Boris GELETIN—launch party of missile department commander (Murmansk Reg.)

16. Senior Lieutenant Sergey UZKIY—target designation group commander (Arkhangelsk Reg.)

17. Captain (2nd Rank) Yury SABLIN—engineering officer (Crimea Rep.)

18. Captain (3rd Rank) Andrey MILYUTIN—damage-control commander (St. Petersburg)

19. Captain-Lieutenant Sergey KOKURIN—bilge party of damage-control division commander (Voronezh Reg.)

20. Warrant Officer Vladimir KHIVUK—mustering technician (Kursk Reg.)

21. Captain (3rd Rank) Alexander SADKOV—combat control commander (Amur Reg.)

22. Captain-Lieutenant Mikhail RODIONOV—computer group commander (Crimea Rep.)

23. Senior Lieutenant Sergey YERAKHTIN—computer group engineer (Murmansk Reg.)

24. Warrant Officer Yakov SAMOVAROV—medical unit chief (Arkhangelsk Reg.)

25. Senior Warrant Officer Alexander RUZLYEV—ship's boatswain (Murmansk Reg.)

26. Warrant Officer Konstantin KOZYREV—electrical navigation group first technician (Murmansk Reg.)

27. Senior Warrant Officer Vladimir FESAK—electrical navigation group second technician (Ukraine)

28. Warrant Officer Andrey POLYANSKY—electrical navigation group third technician (Krasnodar Reg.)

29. Warrant Officer Sergey KISLINSKY—launch party of missile department technician (Kostroma Reg.)

30. Warrant Officer Sergey GRYAZNYKH—computer group technician (Arkhangelsk Reg.)

31. Seaman Dmitry MIRTOV—steering signalman (Komi Rep.)

32. Petty officer (2nd class) Dmitry LEONOV—steering signalmen unit commander (Moscow Reg.)
33. Senior Lieutenant Maxim RVANIN—electrical technical group engineer (Arkhangelsk Reg.)
34. Seaman Andrey DRYUCHENKO—electrician (Arkhangelsk Reg.)
35. Senior Lieutenant Aleksey IVANOV-PAVLOV—torpedo officer (Ukraine)
36. Warrant Officer Viktor PONOMARENKO—sonar group technician (Ukraine)

Compartment 3

1. Captain-Lieutenant Dmitry REPNIKOV—second-in-command (Crimea Rep.)
2. Captain (3rd Rank) Andrey RUDAKOV—signal officer (Moscow Reg.)
3. Captain-Lieutenant Sergey FITERER—automatic space communications group commander (Kaliningrad Reg.)
4. Captain-Lieutenant Oleg NOSIKOVSKY—classified automatic communications group commander (Kaliningrad Reg.)
5. Captain-Lieutenant Vitaly SOLOREV—equipment party of damage-control division commander (Bryansk Reg.)
6. Captain-Lieutenant Sergey LOGINOV—sonar group commander (Ukraine)
7. Senior Lieutenant Andrey KOROVYAKOV—sonar group first engineer (St. Petersburg)
8. Senior Lieutenant Aleksey KOROBKOV—sonar group second engineer (Murmansk Reg.)
9. Senior Lieutenant Alexander GUDKOV—radio intelligence group commander (Kaliningrad Reg.)

10. Captain (3rd Rank) Vyacheslav BEZSOKIRNY—chemicals service chief (Ukraine)

11. Senior Warrant Officer Igor YERASOV—cryptographer (Voronezh Reg.)

12. Senior Warrant Officer Vladimir SVECHKARYEV—classified automatic communications telegraph operator (Nizhny Novogorod Reg.)

13. Senior Warrant Officer Sergey KALININ—missile department classified automatic communications telegraph operator (Ukraine)

14. Senior Warrant Officer Igor FEDORICHEV—control department technician (Tula Reg.)

15. Warrant Officer Maxim VISHNYAKOV—target designation group technician (Ukraine)

16. Warrant Officer Sergey CHERNYSHOV—space communications telegraph operator (Crimea Rep.)

17. Warrant Officer Mikhail BELOV—sonar group technician (Nizhny Novogorod Reg.)

18. Warrant Officer Pavel TAVOLZHANSKY—sonar group techinican (Belgorod Reg.)

19. Senior Warrant Officer Sergey VLASOV—radio intelligence group technician (Murmansk Reg.)

20. Warrant Officer Sergey RYCHKOV—chemicals service technician (Uzbekistan)

21. Petty Officer (2nd class) Yury ANENKOV—missile department mechanic (*Kursk* Reg.)

22. Seaman Dmitry KOTKOV—missile department mechanic (Vologda Reg.)

23. Seaman (backup) Nikolai PAVLOV—missile department mechanic (Voronezh Reg.)

24. Seaman Ruslan TRYANICHEV—bilge mechanic (Vologda Reg.)

Compartment 4

1. Senior Lieutenant Denis KIRICHENKO—damage-control engineer (Ulyanovsk Reg.)
2. Captain Aleksey STANKEVICH—medical service chief (Ukraine, St. Petersburg)
3. Warrant Officer Vitaly ROMANYUK—surgeon's assistant (Crimea Rep.)
4. Senior Warrant Officer Vasily KICHKIRUK—medics team petty officer (Ukraine)
5. Senior Warrant Officer Anatoly BELYAEV—senior ship's cook (instructor) (Ryazan Reg.)
6. Chief Petty Officer of the ship Salovat YANSAPOV—ship's cook (instructor) (Bashkortostan Rep.)
7. Seaman Sergey VITCHENKO—cook (Leningrad Reg.)
8. Seaman Oleg YEVDOKIMOV—cook (Kursk Reg.)
9. Seaman Dmitry STAROSELTSEV—bilge seaman (Kursk Reg.)
10. Seaman Alexander KHALENO—turbine operator (backup) (Komi Rep.)
11. Seaman Aleksey KOLOMEITSEV—turbine operator (backup) (Komi Rep.)
12. Seaman Igor LOGINOV—turbine operator (backup) (Komi Rep.)

Compartment 5

1. Captain (3rd Rank) Dmitry MURACHYOV—main propulsion division commander (Crimea Rep.)
2. Captain-Lieutenant Denis PSHENICHNIKOV—remote control group commander (first) (Crimea Rep.)
3. Captain-Lieutenant Sergey LYUBUSHKIN—remote control group commander (second) (Nizhny Novgorod Reg.)

4. Captain (3rd Rank) Ilya SHCHAVINSKY—electrical division commander (St. Petersburg)
5. Captain-Lieutenant Andrey VASILYEV—equipment party of main propulsion division commander (Crimea Rep.)
6. Captain (3rd Rank) Nikolai BELOZYOROV—electrical-technical group commander (Voronezh Reg.)
7. Senior Warrant Officer Ivan TSYMBAL—electrician (Ukraine)
8. Warrant Officer Oleg TROYAN—chemical service technician (Azerbaijan)
9. Senior Petty Officer Alexander NEUSTROYEV—electrician (Tomsk Reg.)
10. Seaman Aleksey LARIONOV—bilge seaman (Komi Rep.)
11. Warrant Officer Vladimir SHABLATOV—electrical technician (Mari El Rep.)

Compartment 5-bis

1. Senior Lieutenant Vitaly KUZNETSOV—electrical service engineer (first) (Novgorod Reg.)
2. Senior Warrant Officer Nail KHAFIZOV—chemical service senior instructor (Bashkortostan Rep.)
3. Senior Warrant Officer Yevgeny GORBUNOV—diesel technician (Nizhny Novgorod Reg.)
4. Warrant Officer Valery BAIBARIN—bilge team of damage-control division head (Chelyabinsk Reg.)

Compartment 6

1. *Captain-Lieutenant Rashid ARIAPOV—main propulsion assistant (Uzbekistan)
2. Warrant Officer Aleksey BALANOV—bilge team of main propulsion division head (Chuvash Rep.)

3. Senior Lieutenant Aleksey MITYAYEV—equipment party of main propulsion division engineer (St. Petersburg)
4. *Chief Petty Officer Vyacheslav MAYNAGASHEV—bilge specialist (Khakass Rep.)
5. *Seaman Aleksey KORKIN—bilge specialist (Arkhangelsk Reg.)

Compartment 7

1. *Captain-Lieutenant Dmitry KOLESNIKOV—technical group of main propulsion division commander (St. Petersburg)
2. Warrant Officer Fanis ISHMURADOV—technical group technician (Bashkortostan Rep.)
3. Petty Officer, 2nd Class, Vladimir SADOVOI—turbine unit commander (Nizhny Novgorod Reg.)
4. *Seaman Roman KUBIKOV—turbine operator (Kursk Reg.)
5. Seaman Aleksey NEKRASOV—turbine operator (Kursk Reg.)
6. Petty Officer, 1st Class, Reshid ZUBAIDULLIN—electrician (Ulyanovsk Reg.)
7. Seaman Ilya NALYOTOV—turbine operator (Vologda Reg.)
8. Petty Officer, 2nd Class, Roman ANIKIYEV—turbine operator (Murmansk Reg.)
9. Senior Warrant Officer Vladimir KOZADYOROV—turbine technician (Lipetsk Reg.)

Compartment 8

1. *Captain-Lieutenant Sergey SADILENKO—remote control group engineer (first) (Ukraine)

2. *Senior Warrant Officer Viktor KUZNETSOV—turbine operator senior assistant (Kursk Reg.)
3. *Chief Petty Officer Robert GESSLER—turbine unit commander (Bashkortostan Rep.)
4. *Senior Warrant Officer Andrey BORISOV—equipment party of main propulsion division technician (Ryazan Rep.)
5. *Seaman Roman MARTYNOV—turbine operator (Komi Rep.)
6. Seaman Viktor SIDYUKHIN—turbine operator (Komi Rep.)
7. Seaman Yury BORISOV—turbine operator (Komi Rep.)

Compartment 9

1. *Senior Lieutenant Alexander BRAZHKIN—remote control group engineer (second) (Crimea Rep.)
2. Warrant Officer Vasily IVANOV—group of electricians head (Mari El Rep.)
3. *Warrant Officer Mikhail BOCHKOV—bilge party of damage-control division technician (Crimea Rep.)

*12 *Kursk* crew members whose bodies were recovered in 2000

INDEX